MILITARY MODELLING GUIDE
TO MILITARY VEHICLES

GUIDE TO
MILITARY VEHICLES

ROBIN BUCKLAND

ARGUS BOOKS

Argus Books Limited
Wolsey House
Wolsey Road
Hemel Hempstead
Hertfordshire HP2 4SS

First published by Argus Books 1988

ISBN 0 85242 958 4

Photosetting by Alan Sutton Publishing Limited, Gloucester.
Printed and bound by LR Printing Services Ltd.
Manor Royal, Crawley, West Sussex, RH10 2QN, England.

CONTENTS

	Introduction	7
1	Small scale kits	10
2	Large scale kits	46
3	Micro armour	64
4	Tools, techniques and materials	67
5	Metal and resin models	77
6	Crew figures and accessories	99
7	Colours and camouflage	106
8	Reference and research	114
9	Summary	127
	Appendices	129
	Index	139

Miltra's large 1/10 Scale T72, made for a special order, and showing the appliqué armour on the turret roof which the Soviet's are using to counter the latest American anti-tank weapons.

INTRODUCTION

Like many modellers, I began putting plastic kits together as a child, without any serious interest. They were simply playthings, unpainted, with transfers stuck-on haphazardly. Yet I was fortunate, as my childhood coincided with the beginning of the hobby of plastic modelling of military vehicles. It was in 1961 that Airfix released their first kit, the Panther. As a result, I have been able to observe the growth of the hobby from then until now. There have been many changes, which I intend to illustrate through this book. While I don't promise to describe every model ever made, at the back of this book, you will find a guide to all the manufacturers I can track down. There are the major plastic kit producers such as Airfix, ESCI, Tamiya, Matchbox etc, and many of the more specialist businesses who are turning out both metal and resin models. As far as I know, this is the first book of its kind to cover these smaller 'cottage industries' who are turning out AFV models all over the world.

Experienced modellers and beginners alike will find this book useful. Further into the book you will find chapters on tools and techniques, on crew figures and on paints and colours. I hope you will find this information valuable, but I have no wish to insist you do things my way. My view of any model is that it should represent not only the real thing, ie the subject, but also the modeller who made it. At shows, it is good to see differences in style of finish and representation. We are not all necessarily good artists, but the important factor is that we should all get enjoyment and satisfaction from what we produce. What I would not like to see is all models finished in the same style. Therefore, I urge you to develop your own style, and use different styles on different models. In this way you will produce something with its own individuality.

Also, many modellers seem fixed on a particular scale and are largely unaware of the possibilities open to them in other scales. For this reason, you will find details here of AFVs that are available in scales that vary from as small as 1/700 to as large as 1/9th. As well as having had an ever-growing collection for many years, I've also been fortunate enough to have been writing 'Small Scale Scene' every month in *Military Modelling* magazine. This has not only enabled me to keep track of a wide range of producers, but also I have had my areas of interest expanded, and I'm glad of it. There is so much available to those of us in this hobby, if only we bother to look.

I sometimes wonder why we are interested in military vehicles. Clearly, the reasons vary from one person to another. For example, there are wargamers who see the models as simply a necessity to put on the gaming table. These are often the people who want ready-made and ready-painted models which they can put on the table without delay. Then there are the ex-servicemen who enjoy creating in miniature reminders of their own past. Perhaps, also, it is to do with the power involved with the machines. Many people like cars and see them as symbols, such as a Rolls Royce, a Porsche or a Ferrari. Well, likewise, the AFV is still the power on the battlefield. There is growing evidence against this, but the tank is still the symbol of victory, and it is the one thing the defender has to concentrate on stopping. The proliferation of man-portable, heli-borne, or yet more dedicated anti-armour vehicles indicate in themselves the importance of the tank. Its period of dominance is still far from over.

While we are looking at the overall picture of our hobby, the matter of prices cannot be ignored. The plastic kit produced by the majors such as Matchbox, ESCI and the like is still relatively cheap. In comparison with many other hobbies, our basic raw materials cost very little. Yet their production costs are very high. To illustrate this, a company can spend £50,000 on simply having a mould made, and that does not allow for the original research, mastering, materials and packaging. But injection moulding means they can produce a model that can extend from tens to hundreds of thousands. In this way they spread the costs over a large number of products. Also, we must remember that by far the bulk of the output is sold to children as simple toys and they are not produced primarily for modellers. This is another reason why the producers may well decide not to invest in what may be *your* favourite subject if they don't feel it would sell.

The result of this is the emergence of the smaller manufacturers, who tend to be modellers (or wargamers) making models for modellers (or wargamers). Whatever material they are made from, their production is quite labour-intensive and they are produced in relatively small numbers, but this is where you are more likely to find that particular vehicle you're looking for. Some are quite simply conversions from commercial kits, while others are completely scratch-built. On the whole, these are real 'cottage industries', mastered and produced by one person, and we will be taking a closer look at many of them later on. One thing you must remember is that the quality of the models can vary enormously. It can vary with the accuracy of the original master, the type of moulding rubber used, the type of resin used, the number of times the mould has been used, and also, most importantly, the skill of the manufacturer.

Yet, for all the years I've been building AFVs, been talking to other modellers, and reading letters and articles in the modelling press, it still surprises me how people are unaware of just how much is actually available. In the last couple of years, the list of available models has greatly expanded. Indeed, at the rate things are moving, there will be plenty of new releases between me writing this and you reading it.

Before we go on, I would like to make the thanks due in any book. Firstly to all the manufacturers featured in here who have given their time to provide examples of their products and information about themselves. Also to the museums who have provided information. Then also to Ken Jones and Argus Specialist Publications, for enabling me to maintain yet another hobby of being able to write as well as model. Finally, I have to say a special thank you to my wife Jeanette for having the patience to put up with me and my models, which do come in danger of taking over the house at times. Also to my mother for typing it. Now, down to the real meat of the subject.

1   SMALL SCALE KITS

The hobby really took off as a result of Airfix releasing their first 1/76 plastic armour kits in the early sixties. Meanwhile in Europe, Roco Minitanks had already started their range of 1/87 military vehicles, a scale chosen to fit in with popular model railway scales in Europe. The habits have stuck. Obviously there are enthusiasts for every scale all over the world, but it is still fair to say that UK modellers have a preference for 1/76 and that 1/87 still has a greater following in Europe than in the UK. Elsewhere, and especially in the USA there seems to be a particular liking for 1/72 scale, the small 'aircraft' scale. While modellers try to stick to one scale or another, many are now prepared to mix their collections, say between 1/76 and 1/72, and others will collect the excellent Minitank range as well. I have also seen many wargames units that mixed vehicles of all three scales, simply in order to field the correctly equipped units.

Another problem is caused by manufacturers, both large and small, who sometimes produce a model which actually ends up mixing the scales within one kit. For example, ESCI's M4A3 is far closer to 1/76 than its stated 1/72. Then there is the Nitto M36 Jackson, which has running gear that is noticeably undersize. Well, you could of course compare them with a set of scale drawings and these are something we will look at later. But even they do not always agree with each other. Sometimes this is because measurements are taken from different original vehicles, which themselves differ as production facilities changed. Also, mould makers can make mistakes which are simply too expensive to correct later on, and with the smaller manufacturers, the rubber moulding process and the differing resins used can lead to shrinkage which cannot be accurately predicted.

The upshot of all this is that, while there are many accurate scale models available, there are many with faults, major and minor. With such a mixture of potential problems, I long ago chose not to worry about such things and leave my own judgement to be based on the old saying of 'if it looks right then it probably is'. I have seen too many articles and letters from people sometimes known as 'rivet counters' which are particular about the odd milimetre or two; If that is your view, then fine, but don't inflict it on everyone else. The idea is to encourage people to our hobby, not to put them off with ill-judged or misplaced criticism.

Although I do not look too closely at every scale dimension, I do look at the overall quality of any kit. How well does it go together? Are there any alternatives and if so which is best? What else could be made from it? How much extra work is necessary to make an acceptable model? Then you need to weigh all these up against the cost and what you want the model for. A serious collector will look differently at some of the more basic, yet cheaper models than the wargamer, who simply needs a number of them on the table for a wargame unit. Those of you who have seen some of the articles written by the late John Sanders may remember his notes on simplified wargame models. With regular handling, any fine detail would soon get broken off.

What, then, is available from the various model manufacturers?

Airfix
We all owe a great deal to Airfix, for producing the first readily available plastic model kits and for supporting the hobby with their sponsorship of Airfix magazine; something I will be looking at further on. Starting with the Panther in the early sixties, they continued to add new releases on a regular basis. Today you can find plenty to criticise of both the Airfix Panther and the Tiger, which was another of their early models. However, this is because we are judging an early 1960s kit by 1980s standards, which personally I don't feel is fair. Would you expect a model you made 20 years ago to be as good as those you make now? Most of us know of the ups and downs of Airfix, and we should be thankful that Humbrol stepped in and that the range is still available to us. My only quibble is that there were some really excellent kits among their later offerings which have still not been re-released. I am sure the problem is that their major customer is the toy market and young children still like to buy the Tigers, Panthers and Shermans that they read about in their comics. For modern interests, their fine little Scorpion/Schimitar can form the basis for conversions in the whole CVR(T) range of vehicles.

One of the early Sherman kits from Airfix.

Other subjects which are currently available are variable. Their Centurion is OK if a little basic, but nevertheless the only one available and therefore ripe for conversion to other variants, such as the Mk 5 used by the Australians in Vietnam, or the 'Ben-Gurion' used by the Israelis. Likewise, their Chieftain is an early type which needs a lot of work to bring it up to current standards.

Two of their better models – the SdKfz7 half-track and 88mm gun and the Panzer IV – are extremely useful, both in their own right and as the basis for a number of conversions. You can add detail to the gun, as there is now plenty of reference material available. The SdKfz7 can be fairly easily converted in mobile Flak mountings, with soft or armoured cabs, troop carrier, survey vehicle and load carrier. Second, and also a German vehicle, is the Panzer IV. This is a good kit which has held up well with age and forms the basis for so many variants built on that chassis.

As far as Allied AFVs are concerned, both the Sherman and T34 are quite acceptable. The Sherman actually features the M4 with welded hull, M34 mantlet and 75mm gun. Their T34 has the advantage of including both /76 and /85 turrets, depending on which you want to use. Also available is the Churchill VII, which for many years was the only model of this important tank. I must say that, as a young boy, the Churchill was the first tank kit I was given, and it nearly put me off for life. Trying to fit all those suspension arms and wheels and getting everything to fit correctly was frustrating. When given a Sherman later, I found out that not all tank suspensions were as bad. Since then, both Matchbox and ESCI have found simpler ways of producing the same effect with, of course, the benefit of hindsight.

However, there are a number of other models which I would rather see re-released. Top of the list must be the three RAF sets – RAF Recovery, RAF Emergency and RAF Refuelling. All featuring two vehicles: the favourite must be the Refuelling set for including the Bedford QL refueller. Softskin vehicles are always in short supply and these three sets form the basis of dozens of not too difficult conversions. It's little wonder that un-made examples now fetch high prices on the second-hand kit market. In the Emergency set, there are the two Austins, the K6 and K2, while

The Airfix RAF Refuelling set with Matador and Bedford QL had many conversion possibilities, and is now sadly missed.

The Airfix RAF Emergency set has two different Austins which have many alternative body variants.

the Recovery set has the Bedford and a Coles Crane mounted on a Thornycroft Amazon. Pride of the three must have been the Refuelling set which had a 6 wheel Matador and the Bedford QL refueller. The cab and chassis of the QL form the basis for a large family of vehicles that saw service in all theatres of the last war. With their obvious appeal to aircraft modellers as well, I am still surprised we haven't seen these again, particularly as I am told the moulds are still safe and well.

Other candidates would be the Morris 6 wheel tractor and Bofors AA gun, the Opel Blitz and 75mm Pak 40, and the Crusader which again featured alternative turrets, as did their Lee/Grant. The only problem with the Crusader is that it was some 3mm too long. This does affect the 'look' of the model but, as it is not the easiest of corrections to make, you might as well live with it.

Two others were a British Matilda and the German Recce set which included an SdKfz222 and *Kubelwagen*. The Matilda was quite good, but there are alternatives from ESCI and Fujimi, so it is not too badly missed. The Recce set is also not missed as this was not one of their best. Fujimi are better.

There are others which are not currently available, some of which are still unique as they came from major manufacturers.

The Universal Carrier and 6pdr AT gun, the Matador and 5.5in gun, Buffalo and Jeep, Quad and 25pdr DUKW, and Stug III with *Saukopf* (Pigs Head) mantlet all fall short of modern kit standards, but remain quite acceptable. Others with more major faults were the M3 $\frac{1}{2}$ track with a bulkhead that should not be there and German SdKfz 234 armoured car with the wrong pattern mudguards for the type that mounted the Pak 40. They should be the same style as on the Matchbox Puma. Nevertheless it can still form the basis for others of the 8 wheel series.

Another pair seldom seen now are the Scammell Tank Transporter and, for the Vietnam enthusiast, the M55I Sheridan. As someone with a particular interest in the Vietnam conflict, it particularly grieves me to be unable to get hold of the Sheridan. A neat little model.

Finally, two which I can never claim to have been terribly struck on are an early Leopard I and a JS III, whose turret was all wrong. In fact, Jeff Spain of Red Star models (see later) produces a correct resin turret which is designed to replace the faulty original.

Having grown up with Airfix models, I find it hard to grasp that a whole generation of new modellers has come along who have not

An example of the old Airfix box-art, here with their Sheridan.

had the chance to get all of that range which has such an important part in the history of our hobby.

ESCI

I have chosen to look at ESCI from Italy next, for a couple of reasons. First, because their 1/72nd range is *all* still available and, second, because they have made interesting marketing developments. I have mentioned that Airfix included alternative turrets in some of their kits. ESCI make the different turrets, but package and sell the different variants separately. This gives more 'different' kits on the shelf and lets the modeller buy just what he wants, with odd parts left over. Only rarely does this fall down, such as in marketing their original Quad now as a Morris Quad – which it isn't. But perhaps their most important development recently has been to solve a problem that has been with us since the beginning, Trackwork. The solution had always been soft vinyl tracks, which had all sorts of problems, including a reaction where they 'melted' any unpainted plastic they touched for a short length of time. ESCI have chosen to use a mix of individual links and varying lengths in the normal injection moulds, which you assemble around the running gear. It is a little more fiddly but very effective and well worth the extra effort. In my opinion, an excellent solution.

ESCI have also continued to release new kits during times when others have ignored the small-scale market. While there have been some WWII subjects such as more SdKfz 251 Hanomag variants, most recent ones are modern. Particularly, members of the M113 and M60 families with M48, Merkava and T62 variants programmed for 1988. With some of these recent subjects, they are reflecting an interest in the Middle East wars, with Israeli types such as Merkava, M48A2L, M60 with Blazer armour and a T62. I do not intend to go through every model in their range as they are detailed in their current catalogue and should be readily available. But to briefly look at some, their Sherman M4A3 is very nice, but actually closer to 1/76th scale rather than the stated 1/72. However the 1/72 scale M4AI with cast hull also includes a basic engine which could produce some interesting diorama ideas, and even a different slant on a wargame if you build in maintenance problems to the scenario. They also do it with the Calliope rocket launcher, yet I have been unable to find any references showing it fitted to a Sherman with a cast hull.

M163 and M113 ACAV variants from ESCI.

Kits of particular note are the Dodge Weapons Carrier, the 25pdr, the Stug III which has either 75mm or 105mm armament, the SdKfz 251 variants and the Panther Ausf G.

The major development for ESCI has been their acquisition by the ERTL company which has resulted in a change of distribution set up in the UK. Coupled with the programme of new releases, ESCI are making large investments in the modelling field which are worthy of our continued support.

Other points of note for the ESCI range are a number of subjects unique to them, including the Pz 35(t), the British Bishop, Pz I *Befehlswagen*, Italian Fiat M13/40 and Fiat 18/75 S.P. There is also a useful accessory set which has sand bags, signs, boxes, etc., which is useful for adding the extra gear so often found adorning AFVs. On top of that, they have taken over Airfix's old position of providing sets of figures to complement their range. Ideal for wargamers, these give a good selection of well-detailed figures at very reasonable prices. Their only problem is being in a flexible polyurethene, which can mean paint flaking off with much use. If they are properly based and carefully handled, you should be able to cope.

One tip for any AFV modeller is to make sure you hang on to the spare transfer sheets from these models. There are two or three alternatives provided which will often produce something useful for later.

Roco Minitanks

What Airfix was to the UK so Minitanks were to Europe. Made in Austria in 1/87th scale, they were designed to fit in with the popular model railway scale. They are not construction kits in the normal sense of the word, as they come ready-assembled. Yet there has been a slight change in that direction over recent years. They also retain a degree of 'toy' value as all the tracked vehicles, which have solid moulded trackwork, have ready-fitted or alternative parts supplied, for wheels to fit under the hull hidden by the tracks. This is useful for wargamers as well, as it enables the model to be pushed around a table. For those who do not like them it is a simple job either to remove them or not fit them in the first place. All the wheeled vehicles have metal axles which give a degree of strength for any handling the model may receive.

New production methods over recent years have led to an increasing amount of details and accessories being included in the models, which a modeller has to glue on. The variety is quite amazing and unthought of only a few years ago. No other kits provide details such as wing mirrors, windscreen wipers, aerial

An updated M110 from Minitanks.

mounts alongside machine guns, jerry-cans, packs and bed rolls. In some cases, there are even pieces which you can add to your spares box (something we will look at later). As an example, their basic M113 APC comes with six sprues* of accessory parts. Some of them even have pieces some people may not notice. The one I have in mind is their MAN 5t truck which has a tow-bar mounted under the body inside the chassis. This, again, could lead to some interesting recovery dioramas and scenarios. Their early models were sometimes quite basic and sometimes quite detailed, and, in one or two cases, looked blatantly wrong. Those early releases were mostly War II subjects, many of which have since been deleted, such as T34's an M29 Weasel, German 8-wheel armoured cars, among others. Some do remain and, indeed, have been updated to current standards, such as the Opel Blitz 3-ton truck.

But recent years have seen a greater concentration on modern NATO subjects and, being an Austrian company, it is no surprise that most subjects feature either German or American vehicles. Within them are a number of fire engines. Though I am not quite clear as to the reasoning behind it all, the modelling of fire engines in Europe is all the rage. I can't say I can drum up quite the same enthusiasm, though the odd one or two can make an interesting addition to any collection. In particular I would quote their Opel Blitz Fire Tender and the Mercedes Benz L500 and trailer. Both of them are full with extra detail parts, including items like wind-screen wipers, wing mirrors, a portable pump to fit in the Mer-cedes trailer and even the Merc symbol to fit on the bonnet! Definitely 'state-of-the-art' moulding. Most recent is the larger Mercedes L4500.

The one real surprise is that they have not bothered to provide any of the potential opposition to their now large range. For 1988 they are announcing a T72 produced for them in the USA, and which I believe is actually the one made by Petner Panzers. While I feel they deserve to be even more popular than they are, they do need to add more than one T72 to provide some sort of balance before more wargamers will take to them. As it is, they do not readily fit in with other scales such as 1/76 because they are so much smaller. This gap is gradually being filled by other manufac-

Sprue: the name for the length of carrier plastic involved with the moulding process, to which all parts are usually left attached for the modeller to remove.

turers but price, detail and availability does not yet come up to the new Roco standards.

An important extra within the Minitanks range, which can be used by enthusiasts in other scales, is their Decal sheets. Covering an increasing range in sizes and numbers, symbols, badges and signs, they are often adaptable for 1/76 and 1/72. You may well find these worth looking at whatever your favoured scale.

Another interesting development this year for Minitanks enthusiasts has come from their UK distributor, Continental Model Supplies, who have had a series of 1/87 Russian figures made which are now available. There are plans to add to these with more figures as time goes on. With luck we may also see some UK-produced 1/87 Soviet AFVs.

As I write, their new Willys jeep model arrived and it even has an engine under the removable bonnet ('hood' for those of you in

Super-fine detail in 1/87 as Minitanks put engine detail into their Willys jeep.

the USA). It is an absolute delight, with detail undreamt of just a few years ago.

I have started with what I consider to be the three most important ranges for the small-scale modeller. What I would like to do now is to look at the different scales and makes that are available between 1/104th and 1/72nd scale. There are quite a lot which I will describe by scale and not by any particular order of manufacturers. (Addresses are given in Appendix 1)

1/104 or 15mm scale

Quality Castings I know of only this one company which produces white metal castings of quite a large number of AFVs, softskins and figures in 1/104th scale. This may seem an odd choice of scale, but it equates to 15mm scale which has been growing in popularity with wargamers for some years. The range covers WWII and modern subjects, with regular new releases. There are over 150 vehicles available and over 30 sets of figures. Perhaps one of the most notable things is that they are produced in the USA. The reason I say this is because there are relatively few AFV producers in the USA in relation to the size of the country and number of armour enthusiasts, compared to the size of the UK and the number of small manufacturers we have over here.

Small is beautiful with the 38t in 1/104 from Quality Castings.

I have seen a selection of their figures and they look quite good. They are clearly cast with plenty of sharp detail. I have only seen three of their AFVs, and the standards vary from poor to superb. The poor one was a T72, which needed a lot of correction to the turret and to the height of the running gear. The hull was actually not bad. Also poor was a Cromwell, but I suspect this was one of their earlier models. It is not a bad model, just a little basic when compared with their really excellent Pz 38 't'. This little model I felt to be an absolute delight. Sharp, well-detailed parts fit well to give a top-class finished item. So long as others match up to this standard, then 15mm (or 1/04) fans will find this range of interest.

Miltra Miltra are a large producer of white metal vehicles, ready assembled and painted, only in 1/100th. They are all modern subjects as, thanks largely to Miltra's efforts, this scale is now widely accepted as a standard scale for recognition models by the armed forces of many countries. They also buy them in very large numbers, as shown by one recent order alone for some 8,000 models.

These models are not cheap, but the real armed forces want accurate models of the latest equipment and the best availability and durability they can find for the most acceptable price. The result is a degree of quality that Miltra do not want to let slip. With the main hulls and turrets and running gear in white metal, they cast finer details such as gun barrels in tin, or now in brass, in order to be more durable against rough handling 'in-the-field'. They are all assembled with solder as, again, this is a more durable joint than glue when faced with rough handling.

A number of vehicles they have available, particularly some British ones, were originally the John Piper range of 1/100 vehicles that were available in the seventies and later acquired by Miltra. While there are still an increasing number of British and American vehicles being added, such as Challenger, Bradley, LVTP 7 variants, and recently the towed Rapier units, by far the bulk of their range consists of Soviet equipment. This is not surprising for a company whose customers expect to find themselves facing Soviet equipment in most imagined conflicts.

I feel it is a shame that Miltra will not make kits of their vehicles available to modellers, but they do not want to compromise on the quality of the assembled models by letting someone come across sub-standard examples assembled by outsiders. While I can

Ready assembled in 1/100, this is Miltra's Soviet Long-Track radar, made in white metal and etched brass.

understand that view, I am not sure I altogether agree with it. Nevertheless, it is well worth modellers keeping an eye on their model listings, as they include equipment which is right up to date, and sometimes in advance of widespread publication on some types. Examples I would quote are the 2S13, a gun/mortar in a turret mounted on the BMP2 Chassis, as described but not named by Steve Zaloga in his book on Modern Soviet Armour; the Blazer type armour added to T64s and T80, and the applique armour as added to the turret roof on T72s.

In order to produce some of the more exotic types, such as radars, they were also one of the first to use etched brass to obtain the right effect. This is used for radars, aerials and details for items such as on some of the mobile SAM launchers. Some of these are listed as 'a' and 'b' where one will be in travelling order and the other will be in firing configuration. Concurrently there are about 130 Soviet items listed, not including the 'a' and 'b' variations. Another recent development has been the addition of 1/100 scale helicopters on Soviet types. Miltra also do a lot more and we will meet them again later on. A very basic range of 1/100 resin models has just been started.

Roskopf From Austria comes the Roskopf range. They do not

Though in 1/100 from Roskopf, these folding bridge sections still look good with Minitanks.

actually quote a scale, but it is nominally 1/100, as with the aircraft kits they also provide. The vehicles are very similar to Minitanks in style, just a bit smaller and lacking some of that fine detail. Again, the older models are showing their age, and unfortuntely there have been few new releases recently. Most of the range are modern subjects and include Soviet items such as ZSU-57–2 and BTR 152 among others. Amongst their most interesting is a fine set of West German bridging equipment. However, there are a few WWII pieces as well. They also have a number of aircraft models that are true construction kits, some of which are Tamiya models, marketed under the Roskopf label with credits to Tamiya. Others, such as a DFS 230 glider, I have not seen and do not know its origin, though the subject is certainly of interest.

1/87
Petner Panzers Encouragingly, another company from the USA which still only produces the T72 in 1/87 as far as I am aware, though there are others planned. Injection moulded plastic and supplied ready assembled with extra detail parts and a basic decal sheet; this is very much in the Minitanks format, and hence I would identify it as the T72 featured on Minitanks 1988 release sheet. Its standard is up to the Minitanks of a few years ago which is still good. It was produced to compensate for the lack of

1/87 injection moulded T62 from Armourtec in the USA.

reasonably priced Soviet equipment as opposition. This, I feel, it does quite well. I look forward to seeing more from this Pennsylvania-based company.

Armourtec Still in the USA, though moving across to California, Armourtec is another business which decided to respond to Minitank's neglect of Soviet equipment. They turned to the T62 and have produced a plastic injection-moulded kit which, for once, you have to assemble yourself. It is a simple model, which does suffer a little from sinkage at some points on the parts, and which you will need to fill and sand flat. Nevertheless, it is a first rate effort and it includes decals for Soviet and Syrian vehicles. They have a number of other vehicles projected, the next one of which should be a BMP 1. I cannot say it is a model without faults, but it is perfectly acceptable and a very good first effort. Like Petner, they are among the few small manufacturers who have gone straight into injection moulding, which is not cheap, and they will no doubt rely on the one vehicle to help justify the investment in the next.

Model Transport A new range started in the UK in 1987, first produced in white metal but recently changed over to resin. First out was the British Army Fox a/c (CVRT(W)) followed by the

Originally in white metal, the BTR 152 has since been produced in resin by Model Transport, in 1/87.

Trident Models were one of the first to release a small scale Challenger – a metal kit in 1/87.

Soviet BTR 152. Future plans include the BM21 and URAL 6x6 truck. My view is that the resin is actually an improvement over the metal as it keeps slightly sharper details. Again it started from someone wanting to expand on the Minitanks range. They also produce a range of 1/87 scale drawings which we shall look at later.

Trident Made in Austria, these are white metal models which largely feature Soviet items, but with other Austrian and NATO vehicles as well. The range includes some particularly interesting ones, such as all the different equipments in a Hawk AA battery, a towed Rapier, an excellent Challenger, plus others.

General
To finish with 1/87, there has also been a range called Nimix from Spain, of which I have seen an example. Unfortunately, contacts there tell me they are no longer in production. A pity, really, as the Spanish Armoured car I saw also included interior detail and was a very neat kit.

My thanks to Bob Morrison who recently lent me some items made in Russia that are obtainable in Czechoslovakia, and which are supposedly 1/87th. That is a bit dubious, and they tend to remind me more of the old soft polythene ones which Airfix used to turn out back in the sixties. Included are an SU85, T34/85 T34/76 and a quite neat little BT7. They are simply not up to current western standards, but you might like to consider trying to get some purely for interest sake.

1/76
Fujimi/Nitto Two Japanese manufacturers actually chose to go into 1/76 AFVs. They have come together now because Fujimi have bought up the Nitto moulds. The original Fujimi range was and still is a top quality product. Among their range are some excellent kits: The Pz 38t and Hetzer, the Panzer I Ausf B and Jagd Panzer I, plus the last two of which include the 75mm Pak 40 as well. Another excellent model is their M4 Sherman, which has the 105mm gun and HVSS running gear. It forms an excellent basis for making the conversion to the Israeli M50 or M51. My real regret was that they stopped adding new models, despite including six silhouettes in one of their catalogues as future items and which, as far as I know, never appeared. A pity, as they were the PzII, Marder II, Wespe, 15cm SIG 33, Gigant and PzI Bflswgn.

Recently they have added the Nitto range to their listings. These are notable for including good amounts of interior detail, with engines, turret baskets, ammunition and breech details and ideal for diorama enthusiasts. Their vinyl tracks are not as good as the original Fujimi types, and they do become very brittle or melt with the running gear if everything is not given a good covering of paint to protect it. One of their particularly interesting models is that Stug III Ausf D. Unfortunately, it suffers along with the other PzIII variants in that the hull top does not fit cleanly on to the

Morris CS8 and 17lber AT from Matchbox.

chassis with suitable clearance for the track, so it can take some fiddling about to get it right. If you have alternative tracks available it will make life easier. Another one of their kits is very useful for the conversion enthusiast. It features a 120mm Nebelwerfer, a 20mm Flak 38 and 20mm Flakvierling, a 4 box 150mm werfer and launching frame. Both the Flak guns can be put on a number of vehicle mountings, an example of which we will see later. The 4-box werfer can be mounted in one of two variations on the French UE tractor, as produced by Gramodels.

Matchbox As with so many of the other major manufacturers, Matchbox have had their ups and downs but, fortunately they are still with us. Their range of both armour and aircraft kits is aimed in two directions. First, there is the children's toy market, shown in armour models by the inclusion of a small diorama base with every model, and by the use of two or three different coloured plastics, giving them some toy value without being painted. Second, they are aimed at the modellers with their choice of subjects. They remain good value for money and have a number of unique subjects. Think in terms of their excellent Sherman Firefly, the Krupp Kfz 69, Diamond T transporter, Churchill AVRE, SdKfz 263 6-rad and LRDG Chevrolet, among others. There are areas where the models are simplified to keep the prices in line with the toy market, but nothing that cannot be lived with.

I have heard people criticize Matchbox in the past, but I think unfairly. Anyone who believes these kits are produced to the finest detail for collectors, is mistaken. They are produced for children and the collector comes a long way down their list. Nevertheless, they make excellent raw material for anyone who wants to take them further. I am looking forward to their Challenger due later this year.

J B Models Amongst our ever growing band of smaller manufacturers, there is just one who manages to produce injection-moulded plastic kits. Unfortunately, they very seldom add new models. As it is, there are just two available – one a long wheelbase Land Rover, the other an American M113 ACAV. They are not without their faults, but they are not bad and are excellent value for money. They are also properly produced, with window transparencies and a decal sheet included.

I shall be referring later to their Land Rover as a basis for use with resin conversion parts.

Cromwell Models Resin models have been around since the early seventies and Cromwell only came on the scene at the end of 1985. Yet I feel I have to deal with them as the first of our many resin producers. The reason relates purely to the fact that it was Gordon Brown's pioneering commitment to polyurethene resin that started a revolution in our hobby.

It all started with an excellent Israeli Merkava which set new standards in detail and survivability. The softer, tougher resin gave a complete kit, including gun barrel, which was acceptable for collectors and resilient enough for wargamers as well.

Unusual World War One Russian armoured cars from Cromwell.

Cromwell model 1/76 M113 Zelda with additional armour plating.

The ZSU-23-4, a unique 1/76 model from Cromwell Models.

As with everything, experience has brought improvements, with finer detail being successfully moulded, resulting in models of really excellent quality. But things have not stopped, as I know Gordon is still looking at new ways of producing an even better product.

I believe there is one other secret to the success of Cromwell Models and that lies in the constant growth of the range. There are now around 100 plus models available, and that number will soon top the 150 mark. On average this means around four new models each month, so by the time you receive one order there is something new to tempt you again. Releases come so fast I find it difficult to keep up with them all.

Some of the notable models in their range, which now covers vehicles from WWI to the present day, are a series of CMP Cab trucks, Warrior IFV, ZSU-23–4, Israeli 'Zelda' with stand-off armour, T54, Dragon Wagon and Challenger among many others. Many of them have been requested by modellers for years and are proving to be very popular. There are a number of WWII models in the range that, although now ungraded, are from the original Eric Clarke – Milicast range, of which more details later. If there is still anyone who has not tried one of Cromwell's models – they don't realise what they are missing.

Red Star As the name suggests, this range from Jeff Spain features mainly Soviet equipment from WWII to the present. This was one of the earliest resin producers, who used to make them in polyester resin, and which started around 1971. There have been some models during that time which have not been too accurate and these have been steadily removed from the lists. However, despite a break in production during the early eighties, Jeff has continued with them, changing over to the new polyurethene resin in 1986. With this change has come improved detail on most models, the addition of gun barrels which had previously been attempted in metal, and a start at including open hatches and commanders figures.

Among this range are interesting items such as the Zis 5 truck, Studebaker $2\frac{1}{2}$ ton 6×6 (both with loads available separately), BT5, JSII and assorted T26 variants, among others. I am pleased to say that Jeff is another one who continually looks to improve his product and each time they come up for re-modelling so new or improved details are added.

Gramodels Here we have another of our earliest resin producers, as Graham Baker started back around 1971. Produced in the original polyester resin, Graham has chosen a different course to find a better alternative to the fragile resin. Although there is excellent fine detail found on these kits, the resin absolutely stinks a house out during a moulding session. Polyurethene resin does also, plus it contains an amount of cyanide, which requires good ventilation and careful use. The answer for Graham since 1986 has been to turn to white metal castings. At first the two materials ran side by side, but towards the end of 1987 Graham finally called a halt to general resin production. It only now remains in one or two special items, notably his excellent Vietnam Riverine craft. The result is that the largest part of the Gramodels' range is not currently available, but all the metal items are and the older resins are slowly being transferred into metal production kits, which will gradually become available in coming years. Another aspect of these recent times has been Gramodels' use of other materials, notably etched brass and their Vietnamese junk, wood dowel masts and vac-formed sails. I shall be talking later about multi-material kits.

The resin range was very good, with items such as Monty's Humber, Staghound, excellent Bedford TM and unusual Swedish S tank. Now available in their metal form are a lovely little RSO tractor, Guy Ant, Polish TKS and French UE Infantry tractor, while there is also a series of guns which includes a German 150mm Sfh 18 that has limber and full 8-horse team with riders and a separate mounted officer. Very notable is that all eight horses of the team are different, giving a much better look to the finished article. Then there is the British 2 lber and a Polish 37mm AT which again comes with a limber and 3-horse team.

German RSO Tractor in 1/76 from Gramodels. Originally part of their resin range, it is now availabe in white metal.

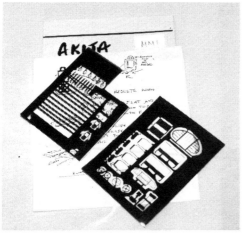

Etched brass accessories in 1/76 from Akita, available via Gramodels.

Milicast – Glasgow This started out as the very first range of resin models by Eric Clarke, originally available only to MAFVA members. Things were rather primitive compared to today's offerings, but basically accurate. They had the first SdKfz 251 Hanomag and PzII available. The range grew and was eventually sold to Milicast in Liverpool and they made an increased range generally available, though still in polyester resin. The range was then sold again in early 1986, to become Milicast-Glasgow with a partnership between Tom Welsh and Cromwell Models. At the same time they transferred production over to the new polyurethene resin. Unfortunately, these arrangements broke up in 1987 and the range was

Horsch Kfz17 radio truck from Milicast, Glasgow.

split between them. It has left a smaller range of Milicast-Glasgow with Tom Welsh but which has begun to increase once again, with both new models and some of the older Eric Clarke ones that have been rebuilt.

Still produced in the polyurethene resin, there is a nice Kfz 17 Horsch Radio Car and an M4A3E2 Jumbo among others. Newer items include M4A1, SdKfz 252 and Canadian G.M.C. armoured truck. Despite the smaller range it is gradually building up again and Milicast remain one of the most widely known brands.

K.K. Castings Distributed through one of the UK's prominent model shops, E.D. Models in Birmingham. Produced in polyurethene resin, there are some very good conversion parts for 1/76 and 1/72 models. Best are the Hard Top, Ambulance and Wire Patrol conversions for the J.B. Models Land Rover. Others are a variety of Churchill turrets to convert the ESCI Churchill and a corrected AVRE turret for the Matchbox kit.

S & S Models One of our newcomers to the resin AFV field, S & S

From S & S Models, two softskins with a French Renault of World War Two, and a modern US M34.

have quickly established the position. They have aimed their product primarily at the wargaming market. The models are cast in older but cheaper polyester resin, with some metal accessories (such as gun barrels). Prices reflect this intention and they are among the cheapest resin models available. Yet they are still remarkably good value for money. They tend to be dimensionally accurate and detail is usually rather basic, though acceptable.

Since starting they have been proved right and their range has been very popular, with continuing improvements in their product quality. A number of unusual subjects include the French FCM 36 and Challenger which have sold widely. They made a brave choice to aim at the cheaper end of the market and they make a very creditable product.

Fent-O-Res Having been around a few years now, Fent-O-Res still use the polyester resin. They are another business where prices are still lower than many others, and they have a very large range of subjects. Unfortunately, they are of greatly differing quality. While there are some that are both unusual and quite acceptable, a fair number, I am afraid, are rather poor. Nevertheless, and provided you compare their prices to others, items such as their Sturmtiger, JSII and SAM8 'Gecko' are perfectly acceptable for the wargaming market. Items which are not so good include their M113 and, supposedly, Australian Centurian. I must say I would like to see them take a close look at their own range and be brave enough to cut out those poorer items.

Jacklex Available through the Harrow Model Shop, a shop which has always been prepared to encourage, and stock, a number of

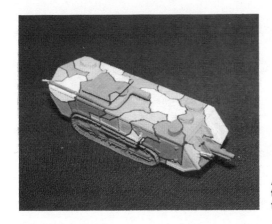

A one-off from Jacklex, the French St. Chamond from World War One.

specialist ranges. They have a large range of metal figures by Jacklex and with them one armoured vehicle. This is most notable for being one of the few models of WWI armour available, and is a French St. Chamond. It is a very good little model and goes together without any problem.

Platoon 20 Another company who are well known for producing figures, particularly those of the Vietnam conflict. Made in Northern Ireland, they also have some vehicles and guns designed to go with their figures. As a result their scale is rather questionable and larger than 1/76. There are M48, M113 and M151 variants, plus guns such as the Soviet M1938 122mm howitzer, and US Pack 75mm, amongst others. They tend to be much simplified but are still quite usable.

Scale Link Among a number of products, Scale Link have a selection of civilian vehicles available in 4mm (1/76) scale for railway modellers, but there is one military vehicle, a Rolls Royce A/C. Though this is the only military model they do in this scale, it is very good. This one is produced as a white metal kit of parts.

Pak 43 Another maker who produces white metal models, and yet has only two models available. Their first release was a well-detailed Pak 43. On a cruciform carriage, this does include crew figures, but does not include the carriage wheels in anything other than an emplaced position. Recently they have added a second model, a German 'Grille' (Cricket), a late model Pz38't' M with Sig 33 in a rear fighting compartment. Well detailed, it includes radios,

The German 15cm 'Grille' (Cricket) from Pak 43 Models.

This Ford WOA2 shows the detail included in the white metal kits from Lead Sled Models.

shells and boxes within the fighting compartment, rather than the usual blank space.

Lead Sled Lead Sled are relative newcomers to the white metal field, yet have earned themselves an enviable reputation. Produced by Dave Cass, the quality and fineness of detail on these models is top quality. They are broken down into almost the same degree that a plastic injection-moulded kit would be. There are two markets for their products, as they do allied soft-skin vehicles plus airfield accessories. One or two of their RAF bomb trollies include some really tiny pieces that are a must for tweezers, and recipe for eye strain if you drop them. Take their tip and put the pieces inside a plastic bag and your hand and modelling knife inside also to do any trimming up. That way these small pieces should not catapult off your work surface.

These are really excellent products and the number of parts makes them what I would call genuine kits, as opposed to single, four or five piece models.

Items within the range include the Dorchester ACV, the Ford WOA2 and Humber 4 × 4 variants, plus aircraft accessories including A, B and C type bomb trolleys, Luftwaffe bomb trolley, Thomson refueller and Fordson N airfield tractor, among others.

Lead Sled models are now distributed by Mil Slides in London.

Ahketon/Lyzards Grin Ahketon are produced by Craig Acheson in the UK, though they also have an outlet through Ahketon USA. Aside from producing a wide range of figures and plaster cast buildings, they have also been quite adventurous in their range of metal AFVs. Not uncommon are items such as Russian T26's, BT7's, M20 and M8 armoured cars, but notably they took on two series which are otherwise largely ignored. There are WW1 subjects with an A7V, Whippet, St. Chamond and Schneider, while from WWII there are some Italian vehicles, including CV33 variants, the AB41 a/c and the P 6/40 medium tank, among others. These also tend to be rather better quality.

They also have the UK production licence for the Lyzard Grin range of figures, guns and vehicles from the USA. I cannot say I find the quality of detail to be too brilliant on this range, but it is perfectly adequate and the range covers a great variety of artillery pieces from all major nations in WWII, and is also notable for having a Katyusha model mounted on a ZIS-5 truck.

Hinchliffe Back in the late sixties/early seventies, Hinchliffe began producing a range of metal guns, plus an SdKFz 251 Hanomag. The range remained static for many years and some of the subjects were overtaken by the plastic kit manufacturers, but others like the German 105mm Lefh 18 and the small 75mm Infantry gun are still unique.

Then, in 1984, they were taken over by Skytrex. Shortly after, they began a rapid expansion to this range of WWII equipment which is continuing today. Still in white metal, here are some excellent kits, like the BA64, GAZ 6 × 4 and 4 × 2 trucks, British 21bers, US 105mm and 155mm Howitzers, 57mm AT and German 37mm Flak and 50mm Pak 38. As with all metal kits, they have the advantage of greater availability due to greater speed of production, which therefore make them popular in the market place. We will see Skytrex again shortly.

Skytrex 20mm scale BA64.

JSII in polyester resin from Ostmodels, in 1/76.

Ostmodels Moving back to resin and, in this case the older polyester resin, we move outside Europe for once. Made in Tasmania, Australia, these are, in my opinion, the best quality models available in the polyester material. In general, they aim at producing kits of the lesser known nations, such as Belgium, Italy and Hungary. Detail and quality is excellent and the finest of parts are included with metal wire reinforcement. The time and effort which Anker Fuhlsburg put into the production of these is clearly evident. Recently they have made an arrangement with Cromwell Models in Scotland, whereby Cromwell will make some of the Ostmodels range in polyurethene resin for the European market, while Ostmodels will produce some of Cromwell's range in polyester resin for sale in the Southern Hemisphere. The material may differ, but the quality remains.

Sunny Staying abroad, let us move on to Japan where Jiro Kadogaki produces a series of SdKfz 251/D variants in a poly-urethene resin, with white metal parts. These are really quite neat, well made and packaged and, of course, are the later D variant. Interesting items include the Pak 75mm equipped 251/22 and the 251/21 A.A. mounting. A bit of work is necessary to get a good fit

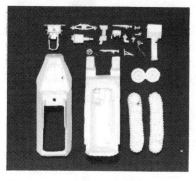

The resin and metal 1/76 kit of the SdKfz 251/9D from Sunny Models in Japan, as you receive it.

The finished Sunny kit of the SdKfz 251/9D.

for the two main body parts. Despite the popularity of the 1/35 armour coming out of Japan, it is especially interesting to see these 1/76 coming out of there as well.

H & S Models Available from Donald L. Squires in California. These actually consist of two ranges which Donald has bought to ensure they remain available to the hobby. Some were originally sold as the Gor-Nig range, and more recently he has added some of the old Zodiac models.

Produced in a clear polyester resin, the rate of production is quite slow as quality is considered of prime importance.

Like many manufacturers, they have some items unique to their range and others which are duplicated elsewhere. Particularly interesting are an Indian Pattern Armoured Car, the Italian Fiat SPA 37 and Morris a/c. Then there is also an M4A3E2 Jumbo, an M18 and an M10 among others.

General

In addition I have heard tit-bits of information about other ranges, such as a Czech producer and another in Japan who use resin bodies with white metal trackwork. Unfortunately I do not have enough firm details on obtaining these. There are also a number of other ranges which are either no longer available at all or have gone out of production, leaving only some items of old stock still available in a few shops.

Gone now for some time have been Raretanks and Modakit,

both UK businesses who had a small number of releases in vac-form kits. This has never been as popular for AFV producers as it has for aircraft modellers, with only two or three large scale kits still using it. They had items such as Cromwells, Kubelwagens, Hetzer and Pz38t. Renown were a small series of metal kits from Phoenix (the figure maker) with a Dingo, Dodge Command and Bedford. The moulds, I gather, have long gone. In resin, Militmen were one of the original series in polyester resin, made by Barry Walby, who has now re-started with white metal Soviet AFVs in 1/72 (see MMS). Very good quality, these are still of great interest among many enthusiasts. Frontline were another large range of polyester resin vehicles but they disappeared after a fire destroyed the moulds. Quality varied somewhat but there were some interesting items. Inkpen/3DFV were the product of Mike Conniford, well known for his scale drawings. They were different for being only available as ready made up and painted. It was a sad day when Mike had to give up for personal reasons, though he has retained all the moulds. This contrasts with Zodiac Models who gave up despite experimenting with both polyester and polyurethene resins, yet sold some of the moulds to Donald Squires in the USA.

GAS was a range available through the Harrow Model Shop, but which is now virtually exhausted. Originally they were made in resin but they later changed to white metal. Here were Saladin and Saracen a/c's, the 1 ton Rover, T55 and T62 tanks. They did the T72 and Abrams in resin, but not in metal, so they are relatively rare now.

In the world of injection moulded kits, there have been two others – Midori had a small series of vehicles that included a friction motor drive unit to give them 'toy' value and were rather basic. Then another was originally known as Edai, from Japan,

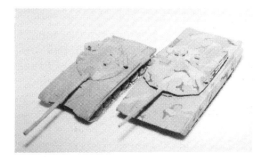

The original T72 and M1 Abrams in resin, from GAS Models.

but they changed the brand name to 'Grip'. One or two of these were disasters, such as their Sdkfz 251 Hanomag, but others like their Mobelwagen and Stug IV were really not too bad. These do stil turn up in the odd model shop from time to time. Track units are all solid, on Minitanks lines, but still acceptable.

1/72nd

Hasegawa Hasegawa, well known for their superb aircraft models, also turned to military vehicles in the seventies. Like others, they chose to create a range and then stop. They chose the larger 1/72 scale in keeping with the aircraft scale. They picked some interesting subjects: the US 155mm long Tom, German Kettenrad, Mercedes 6 x 4, and US GMC 6 × 6 2½ ton truck.

Something of a surprise in my opinion were the two versions of the Karl Morter and the Leopold railway gun. They certainly make for something different.

Heller A little known series of 1/72 AFVs were produced by Heller, though they are not currently listed. However, you can still find them occasionally. They have the AMX30, the AMX 13, DCA 30, DCA 13 and a Somua S35. They are not bad but the detail is not as crisp as one might like. Nevertheless interesting subjects, especialy the AMX 13 which has seen action in Israeli hands and which can make an interesting Egyptian conversion by mounting the turret onto a Sherman hull.

PP Aeroparts First of the smaller manufacturers in the UK, they only have the one model available at present, but it must be the most incredibly detailed one on the market. They specialise in making etched brass aircraft accessories and, as a further extension of that, the Eager Beaver Forklift truck. This little model features 48 parts in white metal, 26 in etched brass, plus rubber tube for hydraulic pipes, copper wire for plug leads (!) and a decal sheet. It is produced in answer to the growing desire to produce the most detailed diorama. I have to say that these are delightful tiny details yet you will need a great deal of patience to see this one through to completion.

Miltra Still in metal, Miltra also have a 1/72 model of the Soviet T72. Not widely available and perhaps not widely publicised. It is not bad and has always been quite reasonably priced.

The resin Horsch and Lorraine Schlepper from Alby Models in France are in 1/72, and highly detailed.

A selection of modern Soviet equipment in 1.72 from MMS: BRDM2; BTR60 PB; MTLB;2S1;BMP2.

A future release from MMS will be this speculative model of the vehicle rumoured to be the 2S13. Only time will tell how accurate this is.

Alby Back to polyurethene resin, these are probably the best you can buy. They are not cheap but the detail and quality is superb. Not only are there complete kits of French, US and German vehicles, there are also conversion sets designed to go with

ESCI's kits. Made by Alain Laffargue, they are notable for having full chassis details as well. My favourite is the Dodge Ambulance, but there are plenty of others. The only problem that arises occasionally is availability. As a serving member of the French Air Force, there are times when duty calls Alain away from production and backlogs do arise. Nevertheless, their quality means people keep coming back. We will see Alby's 1/35 models later.

Verlinden Productions So well known for their 1/35 scale products, there are currently two 1/72 aircraft accessories in the form of US Carrier Deck Tractors. Polyurethene resin, optional parts, instructions and a rub-down decal sheet mean these really are complete kits. There are plans for further additions in this scale during 1988.

MMS Briefly mentioned earlier, this is a range of modern Soviet equipment in white metal. Produced by Barry Walby, there are families of vehicles building up. Variants are already available for the BMP2 and BMP1, BRDM2's MTLB and BTR 60. They include the PRP3 battlefield radar vehicle to go with their 2S1, 122mm SP gun. For the future, they include up-to-the-minute items such as what is believed to be known as the 2S13 (a BMP2 chassis, turret mounting a gun morter such as on the 2S9).

They are especially notable on two counts. Firstly, they are, in my opinion, the best quality metal castings to be found in any models, where detail is crisply captured. Secondly, they are properly packaged in a sturdy box and foam, with instructions and exploded assembly diagram. The result is a well-presented product that reaches you in the same good condition as when it was made, unlike those in flimsy polythene bags that get bashed around in transit.

Airmodel From West Germany – we will be meeting them again later. They produce a series of 1/72 resin vehicles. I have not seen these myself, but someone I know has them all, though has mixed reactions. Some, I gather, are good and scale-up well as 1/72nd, while others are a little mixed in places. In the UK they suffer from conversion-rates from Deutchmark to Sterling. Unfortunately, they work out to be fairly highly priced, especially as they do not include subjects that are not available elsewhere, albeit in 1/76. If you are particular about collecting 1/72nd, then these will be for you. Models include BA6, BA10, BA64 a/c's, BT7, T60, T28, ISU 152 and 122.

Firefight 20 Produced by Skytrex, this is their range of modern equipment, while Hinchliffe covers WWII.

Skytrex started in 1972 to market the products of many small firms then supplying the wargame hobby. This soon changed as they moved into manufacturing their own products. There have also been changes in its management, but it has left one of the four original directors, John Hammond, in control.

They started producing the Firefight 20 range during 1983/4. It was shortly after this, during 1984, that Skytrex purchased the Hinchliffe product lines. They have continued to expand the list, with items such as Hummer variants, Merkava, T55, 62, 72's, Sheridan, V100 and others; including modern artillery pieces such as the British 105mm Light gun. Strangely the quality of these can be a little variable. Their new LAV 25's are very neat, yet their earlier Bradley does not go together without a bit of fiddling about. Nevertheless it is a deservedly popular list, which continues to regularly expand.

Maquette D'Auzi A small business in France who produce aircraft accessories. They have aircraft carrier deck tractors for the US, French and Royal Navies, and have added US fire tenders and stake-trucks to them. In the polyurethene resin they are really made for aircraft diorama enthusiasts, but they are still interesting.

General
I am sure that there are a few small scale ranges that have escaped me and I am always looking out for new manufacturers, wherever they are. Having said that, there are already more than

The LAV25 in the Firefight 20 range from Skytrex.

enough models available to keep a person happily modelling for a lifetime, and which would require more storage room than the average home can cope with. Yet there are still models that people cry out for and, no doubt, we shall see this cry being answered. We have spent years listening to people say that the small scale hobby is dead, but frankly I feel justified to say we have never had it so good.

2 LARGE SCALE KITS

As with so many things in recent years, the production of new models has slowed considerably as the economy of recession hit the world. For the likes of Tamiya etc. to produce a new model requires a huge investment. As a result there has again been a view that the hobby is failing, whereas it is more likely to be the effects of children wanting transformers or electronic games in place of models. One fashion that did come and go is where I would like to start.

1/48

BANDAI A Japanese company, produced quite a large range of AFVs in this scale in the late sixties and early seventies. Just a few can still be found produced in the USA. The scale was first made popular by aircraft modellers, and found a niche between the small size of 1/72 and greater detail of 1/32nd. Likewise, so did these vehicles. If anything, detail was even better than their larger-scale cousins, as they usually included engines and interior details even in the armoured vehicles. Quality was excellent but somehow the range did not really take off. In recent years 1/48 aircraft have become widely popular again and I wish Bandai would try again, as certainly I would buy them. My regret is that I do not have more than the five that are in my collection. There were a variety of Shermans, Stugs, a Hanomag 88mm, SdKfz 7, Austin K5, Daimler a/c and, of course, a jeep, among others. Keep an eye out for any – they are worth it.

Promods In the UK, Promods produce diorama accessories in resin and one designed for 1/48 aircraft modellers is the M151A1 Mutt. The parts do require some cleaning up and you do need to put some work into it to get the best results. Nevertheless, it is

An example of large scale kits, this is ESCI's 1/9 scale Harley-Davidson.

1/48 Wespe from Bandai.

An excellent 1/48 Kubelwagen by Bandai, unfortunately now difficult to find.

basically acceptable and a good effort for something different.

Tamiya For many years Tamiya have had a small assortment of 1/48 AFVs. I think it is fair to say they have been largely ignored by the hobby as a whole. It is reflected in that the range has not been enlarged. Very much on normal Tamiya lines, in terms of quality, but includes interesting items such as the M60A1 and Swedish S-Tank. They are not currently listed I believe.

Aurora This is about the oldest of any plastic AFV range. Produced in line with 1/48 scale aircraft that were initially popular in the USA, these were really not too bad. You must remember, of course, that they were made nearly thirty years ago and are therefore not for comparison with today's products. They can still be found occasionally in hobby shops. Included items such as the Long Tom, Sherman and Centurion.

LRDG Chevrolet from Tamiya, from the author's collection.

Tamiya have re-released their M113 with ACAV shields and new accessories and crew figures to increase demand for one of their older kits.

1/40th

Revell I have never found out why, but Revell chose this unusual scale for a few military vehicles back in the 1960s. There was a Sherman, a 6 × 6 truck and, more unusual, an M56 SPAT Scorpion. In their time they were not a bad product, just such a strange scale.

1/35th

Tamiya I suppose I had to start here really. Although they came after an established 'British' scale of 1/32nd, the Japanese chose 1/35 and have since, due to slow production of 1:32 scale models turned it into the most important of the two. In the early days, the kits were all motorised but their prices at that time put them out of the reach of many of us. Then they changed. Two early kits were a Kubelwagen and a Schwimwagen, unmotorised and relatively cheap.

From there it blossomed. They still produce some with motorised units, but now they come without. Prices have gone back up, but then the detail has greatly improved. No longer are they basic vehicles and now there are crew figures and accessories in plenty to encourage us to build dioramas. An excellent example is their recent M113 ACAV, which includes 'captured' Soviet weaponry, and even beer cans and cigarette packets, complete with decals. To go with them, separate sets of figures have also been produced, even a set of farm animals.

With the large number of kits they have now produced, it is

An example of a recent Tamiya kit, the large LVTP7A1.

difficult to keep all of them in production at once. Fortunately they do keep up by doing short runs at regular periods, so most can be found somewhere.

On top of an excellent product, they currently have the best marketing arrangements as well. Widely available in model shops, with window posters, regular features in the hobby press and, more recently, with a showcase in the form of their own glossy magazine. It is a high profile which keeps the name to the fore. Also, the kits form an excellent basis for super-detailing and conversion. As we shall see later, recent developments have also brought these within the capabilities of even the less experienced modeller. As it is, we have much to be thankful to Tamiya for, in making our hobby what it is today.

Italeri This time from Italy, as the name suggests. Italeri have a prominent place with their 1/35 armour. In many ways I have to say that the detail included in many of their kits is far finer than Tamiya produce. I grant you that there are some ten years between their production but look at the BMW 750 m/c combinations from the two manufacturers. The Italeri kit has the full set of exhaust pipes from the cylinder heads, the mudguard supports and indeed the correct m.g. mounting for the sidecar.

Among interesting items in the range are the M32 Recovery Vehicle, SdKfz 234 Puma, M109 and M24 Chaffee. These last two come in very useful if you want to venture beyond WWII and into S.E. Asia. The Chaffee in particular was used in Vietnam by both the French during the early fifties and onward by the ARVN for many years more.

In recent times they have also taken over another set of moulds. These started with Max in Japan, to Airfix in the UK and on to

Italeri. The only difference now is that the trailers that were included with the Dodges, the 6 pdrs with the Bedford Portee and the *Nebelwerfer* with the R80 are all now sold as separate kits. Despite their age, these still compare well with currently produced models. Among my favourites are the German RS0 (*Raupen Schlepper Ost*) and the Dodge ambulance.

Their accessory sets are excellent (weapons, tools, jerry cans, etc.), but figures are always too much on the skinny side and rather poor.

ESCI At the time of writing, ESCI have had a few 1/35 items on the market but have recently announced some unexpected additions. Like so many other makers, they have recently been sold and were bought by ERTL from the USA which makes these new announcements so much more unexpected. There will be Abrams and Leopard II variants, plus the Soviet T72 and T74M.

Their older kits are also highly detailed and with some unusual subjects. There are the SdKfz 10 Demag, plus the Flak variant, and, more unusually, two pieces of German horse-drawn equipment, a general service wagon and an ambulance. Like Tamiya, they also have various figure sets, but I must say I do not feel them to be as good, as the basic anatomy lets them down.

Heller These are not really as sharp in terms of quality as other kits, but they hold interest for covering French subjects, not just post war items like the AMX13 and AMR but also the Somua S35, Renault R35 and Hotchkiss H39 tanks from WWII. Unfortunately, availability is not all that perhaps it could be, so you will have to keep your eyes open for the ones you want.

Nichimo Back to Japan, and Nichimo have a fairly small range of AFVs. Available with and without motors, their Tiger I is marginally better than the Tamiya version. They also have Jagdpanther, Elephant, Panther and King Tiger available.

Nitto They also have a small number of 1/35 vehicles available, originally produced some years ago. Since the sale of Nitto, I frankly do not know what has happened to the moulds or whether Fujimi have them as well. Not up to present-day standards, their tracks were a continuous rubber band. Of interest was the subject matter. They had an LVTP4 Alligator, M4 Artillery tractor, plus an

SdKfz 251 AusfA mounting the 150mm rocket frames. They can still be found in a number of hobby shops.

Spojnia A new manufacturer to us in the West, this Polish company have just one kit so far, a Polish 7TP. Based on the chassis of a Vickers design, the same chassis was used for the Soviet T26 series, all of which are therefore conversion possibilities. Unlike many products from the Eastern Bloc, this is really of a standard that matches what we were producing here in the West only a few years ago. From what I have seen of it, this would be well worth getting. There are now a number of stockists for this kit here in the West.

Tauro An Italian company, there is only one kit so far as I know. It is especially interesting for being a WWI subject, which is something of a rarity in 1/35. Their German A7V is a good model and includes interior detail. It has been out for some years now and is still available from a number of hobby shops. This can make an interesting display of models if you had the A7V, which had a crew of 18, alongside Panzer I through to VI, and the current Leopard II.

Scale Link Produced by John Piper, who we met earlier with 1/100 scale, he now has a series of white metal and etched brass products for the railway modeller plus 54mm WWI figures and equipment. The larger items of equipment include a French FT17, a Rolls Royce a/c, and some artillery pieces. These are very detailed, though as with most white metal models, quite highly priced. Assembly techniques can be slightly different and we will look at these later.

Sovereign Produced by John Tassel, this is one of a number of producers who have realised the possibilities presented by using polyurethene resin. They have in fact combined that with using white metal for smaller detail parts. Currently there are two available, a Humber MkI a/c and more recently the German SdKfz 231 6-wheel a/c. They are available through Historex Agents in Dover, rather than direct from the manufacturer. Future items are due to include a Daimler a/c.

Miniature Military-Models This series is made by Jon Bottomley and produced in polyurethene resin in association with John Tassel. The first release was seen at Euro Militaire in 1987, a fine

This polyurethane resin V100 in 1/35 is by Miniature Military Models.

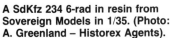

A SdKfz 234 6-rad in resin from Sovereign Models in 1/35. (Photo: A. Greenland – Historex Agents).

model of the V100 Commando. Again it is basically in resin and with white metal details. Second release is also a modern subject, a British Ferret a/c. It makes a pleasant change to see a British vehicle added.

Accurate Armour Made by Derek Hansen and moulded by Gordon Brown. I would consider this to be about the foremost maker of complete 1/35 kits in polyurethene resin. Their first release was the Soviet BMP 1, which set new standards, and showed just how much can be achieved. In their later BTR 60, the grab handles are moulded with the hull and are hollowed out, at most leaving some fine flash to be cleaned away. That these can be consistently produced says much for the quality of their production techniques.

Since that first release, they have continued to add interesting new models and maintain an excellent quality. Prices are obviously higher than injection moulded plastic kits, but the finished article compares well with them for crisp detail and it reflects the work put into hand producing something in small numbers for enthusiasts instead of commercial mass production.

They have also turned their hand to accessory parts. For example an Urdan cupola for M48 tanks, and the ACAV guns and shields to upgrade the basic Tamiya M113 kit into the ACAV. While it was unfortunate that Tamiya chose to upgrade their model into the ACAV themselves, it shows the risks that small manufacturers face when investing time and money into something that others may be doing. In this case, however, it enables modellers to update M113's that they have purchased in the past.

Resin conversion kits such as this set of ACAV shields can update the original Tamiya M113.

Cast resin conversion parts from ADV in France.

The 1/35 Sherman conversion from ADV.

A.D.V. This is one of a group of resin manufacturers from France. They produce a number of excellent conversion sets for the Tamiya and Italeri Sherman kits. A.D.V. make both hulls and turrets in polyurethene resin. Very good quality, there are fortunately a number of hobby shops that stock them though they are sometimes in short supply. In addition, there is a complete kit available in the form of a Soviet T60. Again it makes up very well.

Before and after – the 1/35 BA64 a/c from Des Resin, in kit form and completed.

The Char B1 bis in 1/35 is a resin kit. The quality is as good as an injection-moulded plastic kit.

This SU100 conversion from Alby simply has replacement parts that match the Tamiya SU85 mouldings.

The 1/72 and 1/35 ranges from Alby Models.

Des Resin Second producer from France, they again use the polyurethene resin and have both conversion sets and complete kits. Their conversion sets include Sturmtiger parts for the Tamiya Tiger 1, the Porsche turret for the same company's King Tiger, and new hull top to make the Hanomag SdKjz 251/1 D variant. Their complete kit is for the little French chenillette Renault 1937R and trailer. Here the resin comes into its own, as the separate flexible lengths can be accurately arranged around the running gear.

Alby On top of his excellent 1/72nd range, Alain Laffargue also has both conversion sets and complete kits in 1/35th. The conversion sets are very good, and I would quote a recent SU100 conversion as an example. To convert the Tamiya SU85, new superstructure top and front plates fit perfectly onto the kit hull and use kit parts for detailing. This kind of quality enables even inexperienced modellers to complete a conversion in this scale.

This is Miltra's basic 1/35 T80, without reactive armour.

This resin BT42 in Finnish markings is from Fairy Kagaku in Japan, in 1/35.

With complete kits, their Char B1Bis has to be one of the finest available anywhere. It is broken down into what I would call a proper kit of parts. Yet their fit is first class, and compares with any plastic kit. The trackwork comes as sections of three or four links which you build up. What puts the whole thing a step above the rest is a decent instruction sheet and a full set of rub down decals. Safely boxed, this is a very complete model. Plans are in hand for at least one more in 1988, which, I understand, will be a Pankard 178 a/c.

Miltra As with their smaller scale ranges, so Miltra do provide 1/35th scale models to their military customers. One of the latest, released in two guises, is still fairly mysterious to us in the West, that of the Soviet T80. The original plans they produced were in turn updated at the last moment when they found the track pattern was wrong. The model was then corrected. It is modelled in polyurethene resin plus some white metal parts. Extra special, however, must be the second version, which features a full array of reactive armour. With all this explosive blockwork it changes the appearance of the whole thing. The models are available in either kit form or fully assembled.

Fairy Models While I have not actually seen one of these models, I have heard good reports of them. These are resin models, made in Japan. There are some interesting and different subjects, such as the Finnish BT42.

M.B. Models Made by Mike Bishop, whose original models have won a number of prizes at I.P.M.S. (International Plastic Modellers

This is how it can look when you have finished with it.

In 1/35, the BTR 60 PB from MB Models in the USA. This is how you will receive this polyester resin kit.

Society) competitions in the USA, this is a series of 1/35 conversions and complete kits, cast in polyester resin. It seems the polyurethene resin is not available there. Complete kits include a BTR60, Char B1 and FT17. Though in polyester, the hull of the BTR60 is hollow, allowing you to have open hatches. There are conversion sets for use on Tamiya's KVI, KVII and T34, to produce early variants, plus a KV85 conversion. Most up-to-the-minute though are conversion sets for the Spojnia 7TP, to make a T26 S and soon an earlier T26 1933. Well packaged in strong boxes, they should survive the post quite well. Future plans include a JS II, T28 and Hungarian Toldi I/II.

Tonda Coming from Czechoslovakia, Tonda turn out Vac-Form kits, specialising in Soviet Softskin vehicles. Some parts, such as wheels, come as resin parts, though these tend to be quite crude in comparison with others. Their vac-formed parts are actually rather good for this particular material. Unlike aircraft modellers, AFV modellers have never really taken to this medium. Equally, the subject matter is unique enough to make these desirable. Availability is a little variable, but there are one or two shops that manage to get hold of them.

Airmodel Produced in West Germany, they have had a number of conversion sets for Tamiya models, but again they are vac-formed. The problems are that sharp corners and fine detail are largely missing. Though these are still available, they have begun to do resin models as well. They are really quite good, even though they are rather expensive by UK terms. There is an 88mm Pak 41/43 which includes many fine parts, all of which use an intentional amount of flash to act as a kind of sprue that holds the parts together. Larger vehicles include the German Wespe 105mm S.P.

Peddinghans Another West German producer, they have both the single and twin versions of the German 128mm A.A.guns. These consist of both metal and resin parts. The twin mounting in particular makes up into a large and impressive weapon. They have also released their first conversion part – a Soviet KV1 tank turret to fit the Tamiya 1: 35 scale kit.

Barton Miniatures A recent development from Barton has been a kit of white metal and etched brass parts, for the British Schimitar CVR(T). Again, it was first seen at Euro Militaire in 1987 and is now available through Historex Agents in Dover. It is very much a kit of many parts and will take a lot of time even for straightforward assembly. Cost is high, but it must take a lot of work to produce a kit like this and its market will remain relatively small. I have not examined one of these, so I cannot say how well it actually goes together.

AEF One of our few producers from the USA, AEF have quite a large range of products. There are one or two complete kits but far more conversion parts. Some are quite good, yet some are rather poor. For example, there are some really useful sets of Israeli Blazer armour and parts to convert the Tamiya Centurian into an Australian variant. On the other hand, the Cadillac Cage turret is considerably out of shape. All in all, not without some faults, but generally includes some very interesting pieces.

Top Brass From here in the UK come sets of accessories in white metal and etched brass. There is the best .50 cal Browning you will find, and the finest set of detail parts for any Sherman tank. More recently they have added sets of tracks which also enable you to produce virtually any variant of Sherman when combined with the M.A.C. (see later) conversion sets to go with the Tamiya and Italeri Shermans. Distributed through Tyresmoke Products they are the work of Tim Perry who also produces that highly detailed Eager Beaver in 1/72.

This is a 1/35 Israeli Centurian with reactive armour blocks, converted using conversion sets by AEF Designs from the USA.

Etched brass accessories from Top Brass on a Tamiya Sherman.

 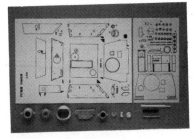

Miniature Armour Conversions produce this T54 conversion turret and engine deck to convert the Tamiya T62.

The K & K Castings 1/35 AVRE turret is notable for having some internal details

Miniature Armour Conversions (MAC) The work of Bruce Crosby and distributed by Tyresmoke Products, these polyurethene resin conversion sets are very good quality. They do a corrected turret for the Tamiya T62 and a set to convert the same kit into the earlier T54. Others include the turret for the M4A3E2 'Jumbo' conversion with templates for you to cut additional hull armour from 30 thou plastic-card. A composite hull top came next and further Sherman pieces are planned.

Above: These pre-printed card and resin parts are in 1/35 from Leo in Japan. This is for their Sturmtiger.

Right: Here is a Tamiya hull with Tiger roadwheels, Leo 'Smallturm' turret and Model Kasten tracks for a Panther II.

K & K Castings Distributed through E.D. Models in Birmingham, there are both T34/85 and Churchill AVRE turrets, jeep tyres fitted with snow chains and an alternative Tiger I cupola. Cast in polyurethene resin, the AVRE turret is not only hollow but includes some interior detail as well.

Leo From Japan, these are conversion sets consisting of resin mouldings for the more complex parts, such as their Kugelblitz turret and pre-printed plastic card where you simply cut the pieces out ready for assembly. A simple, yet effective idea, these are the only products I know of using this system.

Model Kasten and Maxim Though only accessories, these are injection-moulded plastic. They consist purely of well detailed individual track-links for PzIII and IV, Panther, Tiger, King Tiger, T34 and KVI. They replace the vinyl kit tracks and are really good. They are to be found in the new Gunze Sanyo hi-tech kits. Just as good are Maxim for Hetzer tracks. Not cheap, but they add that finishing touch for the real enthusiast.

Miley Conversions Bill Miley in the USA produces resin conversion sets, with T62 turrets and T34/85 turrets among other pieces. These are well detailed, and another of the few sets of products from the USA.

Perry Vac-Form There are six sets of Sherman conversions pro-

Dioramas are about the most popular way of displaying 1/35 models like this Italeri M7 Priest, by Francois Verlinden.

Maxin injected-moulded track links installed on an Italeri Hetzer.

Unfinished to show the component parts, Verlinden's Sherman and wading gear on the Italeri Sherman chassis, including etched brass accessories.

This 2cm Flak 30 is a simple metal gun kit in 54mm scale from Hinchliffe.

duced in Holland. In addition to the vac-form parts there are also white metal accessories. They go with both the Tamiya and Italeri Shermans and enable you to produce most variants. Detail is adequate, though the metal mouldings are rather crude compared to others. Not bad, though resin alternatives have come along since.

Verlinden Productions Probably one of our hobby's best known names; it is no longer fair to consider this a small manufacturer. There is now a huge product range, which includes some Sherman conversions, most notably being the Firefly and one with the Wading equipment added. Other useful accessories which are especially armour related, are sets of well detailed rounds of ammunition and ammunition boxes. On top of all this and many other items, they also produce sets of rub down decal sheets.

Verlinden has been very much a success story and indicative of the popularity of these specialist products.

1/32

Hinchliffe Now produced by Skytrex, there are a number of white metal artillery pieces, including the German 105mm Lefh18 and Pak 38 50mm AT gun. Pride of place, however, must go to their 150mm Sfh 18 which is obtainable complete with limber and 8 horse draught team. Available for a time under the Caldercraft label, this is very impressive indeed. We will see their 105mm shortly as an example for assembling a metal kit.

Airfix Lovely models, but their choice of 1/32 scale was outpaced by the Japanese products in 1/35. You can still find some; they produced the Lee tank, British Crusader, Monty's Humber and Rommel's command half-track, an Sdkz 250 named 'Grief' and finally a 17 pdr AT gun.

Monogram This is a small range of kits which Monogram first produced some years ago. Though in this scale, they were helped by the superb dioramas produced for them by Shep Paine. While the jeep, Sherman, Brumbar and PzIV have been done in 1/35 by Tamiya, Monogram are still the only one to do the amphibious M29 Weasel.

On the Mark From the USA, On the Mark make etched brass accessories for detailing Tamiya kits, and barrel rifling for various weapons. These are quite good, though not up to the standards set by Top Brass products. However, these subjects are welcome, with details for Challenger M48, M60 among others.

Cesare Gambari:/GA., RE Models s.n.c. Made in Italy there are conversion parts in polyurethene resin. An AA turret to convert the Italeri Crusader and welded M3 turret to make the 'Honey'. There is also a set of punches to produce Zimmeritt on plaster or milliput (A and B modelling compound).

Gunze Sanyo These are Hi-Tech armour kits, with major components in plastic, white metal and etched brass details, turned brass gun barrels and the Model Kasten track links. This is

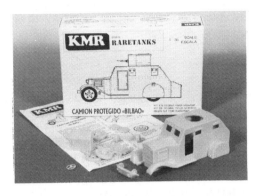

KMR 1/35 resin models from Spain.

an answer from major manufacturers to the market of expensive but highly detailed models for the more limited collectors' market.

Aeromodel Made by W.K.Resin in West Germany, this is a small range of AFVs. There is a VW lltis, a BRDM I and BRDM 2. They are in yet another form of polyester resin, and there is good detail. The lltis is reasonably priced and in my opinion would make quite a good one for beginners, with a neat end result.

K.M.R. Produced in Spain, this is yet another series in poly-urethene resin, though the quality of detail tends to be a little crude. Subject matter is quite interesting, with Italian CV33, Soviet BA 10 and BA 6, French FT 17 and two armoured vehicles from the Spanish Civil War. Again there are one or two shops stocking these which enable you to check availability first. They form the basis for a good model provided you put work into them yourself.

General
At the time of writing I have heard bits and pieces of information about some other products/producers coming on to the scene. E.D. Models are working on an AEC a/c. In the USA there are Schmitt-Vac models available from a couple of sources, but of which I have not had any details. In Korea, Academy/Minicraft are producing what are apparently ex-Tamiya moulds.

There are and have been kits in larger scales. A Russian company, Orgainek, have a few 1/30 scale AFVs, though frankly these injection moulded models are way behind the standard we now expect.

Up to 1/25 scale you will find a small number of models

available from Tamiya. Probably the prime and most well known one among them is their Tiger I, with interior detail. In fact there is still a fair amount missing but it is a good project for anyone wanting to superdetail a kit. Further up to 1/16 and you come to Tamiya's radio-control kits of a Sherman, Leopard and Gepard AA tank. At the same scale, Bandai's small number of models today fetch high prices on the collectors market as they are not currently produced.

Imai also did an Elephant but this was a very high cost kit, designed for radio control.

At the top for detail is ESCI's series of 1/9th scale motorcycles. Many of you may remember Bill Hearnes superb scratch-built figures that went with the BMW combination and the Harley Davidson. Beyond the bikes there was both a Kettenrad and a Kubelwagen. There is a lot of work in these, but the end result is really very impressive.

For the ultimate large scale modelling project, Miltra have produced a 1/1 scale, yes, full size, model of the Soviet T80. Somehow I cannot see my wife letting me try that in the back garden.

3   MICRO ARMOUR

Beyond the scales we have looked at, you can go a lot smaller. Aimed primarily at ship modellers, Skywave are a Japanese producer who make small ships, landing craft and vehicles in 1/700th scale. Though these injection moulded models are tiny, they still consist of about 4 parts (hull, turret and track units). There are Shermans, LTV's, Dodge 6x6's, T34's and JSIII's on the Allied side, Tiger, Panther PzIV, Hanomag, and 88mm on the German, among others. Combined with the landing craft they offer some interesting diorama or even wargames scenarios.

Moving up slightly, Miltra do a small series of 1/500th models. There are around 15 models, including Tiger, 251/D, Firefly, T34, 17lber, BMP, and T72.

Then, 1/300 is a very popular wargaming scale. You can get realistic ranges and 1 to 1 units on to a gaming table. In the early days, they were often crude lumps of metal. Skytrex, who have another series in this scale, have completely re-vamped their range in the late 1970s. One of the leading companies since this scale first started has been Heroics & Ros. This has always been full of fine detail and you can build an intriguing collection with these, even if you are not a wargamer.

A recent newcomer to this scale are Scotia Micro Models. First made in resin, these are now only available in metal. One or two of the earliest models were a bit poor, but most of them, plus all the more recent ones, are rather good. They have particularly added extensive ranges for WWII Japanese and Modern Chinese and French forces.

Even more detailed models are produced in the fractionally larger scale of 1/285 by two companies in the USA. One from GHQ and also licence-produced in the UK by Minifigs. The other one, C & C Castings, also in the USA. I do not know how GHQ are able to get quite such fine detail on their castings, though I am told

Mini diorama featuring card houses with Heroics and Ros M60A3 and M577 in 1/300 scale.

1/300 Bergepanther by Heroics and Ros.

C & C are marginally even better, but I have had no response to my enquiries there, so I cannot confirm it at the time of writing. Finally we come down to 1/200th. This is actually quite an old scale, as I understand that German forces during the last war used 1/200 models for wargaming planned actions. Today, Sky-trex have a rapidly growing range of excellent value models which are gaining in popularity. Recently they have produced some decal sheets to go with them.

Moving to the Continent, Trident Models in Austria produce a good quality series of metal models in 1/200th, but these are all modern subjects. Not far away in Germany, Mercator make a number of WII subjects, and these are different for being available ready painted. One or two of these are not very accurate, but others are really very good.

Micro-Armour was really created for wargamers, and attendance at most wargaming shows normally includes at least one game in this scale. These will often show you how much can be

1/285 GHQ Microarmour, with Leopard II, Challenger and Chieftain.

These 1/200 models are examples of a collector making models for himself. This Karl and Munitionspanzer are from Ron Crawford in Canada.

done with these scales and the tables look very good. With all the detail now being included on these castings, a good paint job pays dividends. As a result, there is an increasing number of people who collect them in their own right. Anyone with limited space can display quite large units, and the huge choice of subjects can give a very varied display. Yet another alternative which I quite like is the diorama potential. With some of the excellent scenic items available now, lots of possibilities present themselves.

While I have no details, I recently discovered that there is a Microscale AFV Newsletter, produced bi-monthly, in the USA, especially for 1/285 and 1/300 AFV collectors and wargamers.

4 TOOLS, TECHNIQUES AND MATERIALS

It may seem odd to leave this so far into this book. The reason is two-fold. Firstly my intention has been to show both new and experienced modellers just how much scope is available to them. Secondly, experienced modellers have their own techniques, while I do not particularly wish to preach to new modellers. My reason for that is I want people to make their own minds up.

I have read too many books and articles which leave the reader with the impression that there is only one way to accomplish something, and which they may be unable to afford or cope with. Therefore what I want to do is throw some ideas into the arena and you can pick and choose as you please.

To start with, if you are simply assembling plastic kits, then all you really need is a tube of glue and a sharp modelling knife. That will always be the basis of any toolkit. Knives and spare blades are not expensive. I have used a plastic handled Swann-Morton craft tool for years. With a selection of straight, curved and hooked blades you can deal with most things. The one thing you must always be aware of is just how you use them. These blades are as sharp as scalpels, and if you are not very careful you will end up slicing your fingers. I must admit to having given myself some nasty cuts over the years, and I urge you to learn from my mistakes. Always cut away from you or on to a firm working surface. There are other more substantial, or even cheaper knives available; it is really a question of deciding what you feel happiest with.

These sharp pointed knives can be used to cut items from sprues, trim away the excess flash, trim off the sprue feed points, to scrape excess dried glue from a join, or to open up holes and hatches if required.

The acquisition of extra tools really depends on what work you want to do.

Basic tool kit of tweezers, tube of glue, craft knives, scissors and pin chuck.

One that I acquired fairly early on was an X-Acto saw. If you want to convert or scratchbuild vehicles, then you will often have large pieces of plastic you need to cut in two, but without using the saw you will destroy a sizeable quantity of plastic in the process. The thin blade of a razor saw will keep this loss to the bearest minimum.

Other items you may well find in the house. In particular, a pair of scissors and a pair of tweezers are always useful – these again are things I have had in my tool box since the early days.

If ever you want to cut out plastic card, then a straight edge is a must. A metal ruler is best, as a plastic or wooden ruler can be cut into by the knife blade, thereby ruining your straight edge and your ruler. I use a metal 6 inch ruler, graduated down to 1/100ths of an inch.

The other gadget I added very early on was a pin-chuck. This is a small hand operated drill for fine drill work. An alternative that can in some respects be easier, is a household pin, held in something like a peg for a handle, and heated in a candle flame. This makes a very 'instant' drill on any plastic. It throws up a rim of melted plastic around the hole and you just have to trim it away with your modelling knife. Just an important word of warning if you do choose to do it this way, do ensure that the candle is firmly fixed by placing it in something like a large lump of plasticine or proper candle-stick holder. Only light the candle when you have to use it and extinguish it as soon as you have finished the job. The plastics and glues we use are highly inflammable, so please, remember to always put safety first – we do not want any fires started.

If you can afford it, then a miniature power drill is a worthwhile investment. There are a number of different makes (Como, Black & Decker and Dremel are the most common) and different grade drills within those ranges. They are powered via transformers from the mains. I would recommend that you pay that little bit extra for a variable speed transformer, as that extra control comes in handy when working with an ever greater variety of materials. These are not cheap, although provided you shop around enough you can often find some amazingly good deals. I do not want to say which is best, because views will differ from one person to another. You may find the smaller drills easier to handle or the larger ones enable you to do tougher jobs. It all depends on how much you want to use it and for what. Again, take a good look around the available alternatives and choose one that suits your own needs, not the salesman's.

Having got the drill, you will find an amazing variety of 'bits' for them. Different size drills, cutting discs, polishers, wire brushes, grinders, etc. all with a variety of uses. These are usually readily available in hobby shops and it is a good idea to experiment on scrap plastic to find out just what can be done with them. If you want to find a cheap supply of used ones for rough work, then get on friendly terms with your dentist (if possible) and ask him if he would be kind enought to let you have any that he may have finished with. They may be no longer of any use for teeth drilling, but normally, there is plenty of life left in them for a modeller.

Adhesives

Once upon a time, military vehicle modelling was easy – all you needed was a tube of polystyrene cement. With the advent of all today's different materials, that has changed. There is now a huge variety of glues/adhesives available which fall into the following categories:

Polystyrene Cement This is the basic ingredient. Theoretically, it works by melting the plastic it touches, which mixes together, so it is securely bonded when it dries out. Its problems are really that it is quite thick and, therefore, can ooze out of a join, get on your fingers, and spoil the surface detail of the model. Excess cement can also melt a part too much and thereby distort it. Sometimes it can also be 'stringy', in other words, leave a fine string of glue as your remove the tube from where you are applying the cement. This can then suddenly break and fall across the model, again damaging the detail when you try to remove it. Nevertheless, used with care it is still extremely useful. Its thickness can also be an advantage, as it has a degree of gap-filling potential. Equally, if some oozes out along a join line, wait until it dries, cut it off with a sharp knife and you will have a neat and very strong join. Whatever some may say, I still use it a lot and find it most effective.

Though some would have you use it on polyurethene resin kits, I am not too keen. It certainly sticks to it, but it does not melt the material to form a decent bond in the way in which it is intended.

Cyanoacrylate Commonly known as 'superglues'. A development from the space programme, this glue provides almost instant bonding, well, about 10 seconds, between most materials. This includes human skin, so be extremely careful when using this. There are de-bonding agents available and it is a good idea to keep some in reserve, or nail varnish remover also works. There are two varieties: For want of a better description, thin and thick. Personally I do not like the thin glue as it tends to run into places where it is not wanted. The thicker type, however, stays where you put it and I have found it provides a much more reliable join. With the thinner type, I have found that its adhesive qualities can deteriorate and a slight knock will cause things to come apart.

It is worse with metal models where weight plays its part. The thicker type does not seem to give these problems so much. It is the best adhesive I have found for using on the new polyurethene resin, for which it gives an excellent join.

On metal models, it is ideal for attaching small parts such as hand wheels etc. It is really a must for attaching the small etched brass parts that are now becoming available, as it will glue them to resin, metal or plastic. I think it is safe to say that this is essential for today's tool-kit.

2-Part Epoxy Adhesive An epoxy adhesive comes in two separate tubes, one being the adhesive and one the hardener. They need to be mixed in what are usually equal quantities to form a paste that is normally a very powerful adhesive. Some have faster setting times than others. Their problem is the setting time, though some do harden in about five minutes, as you have to keep the parts correctly positioned while it sets. It does leave you with a good strong join and is especially useful on large metal parts or on dissimilar materials.

Clear Glues Again, there are plenty of makes, but glues such as *UHU* and *Bostik* are available. This is a general-purpose adhesive, useful for card and paper, or for joining say metal figures to a card base.

Wood Glue (PVA) This white glue, which can be easily diluted in water, is ideal for scenic work, fixing ground scatter, or foliage in trees and bushes. It has the advantage that, though it is white, it dries perfectly clear, leaving just the colours of the scatter to be seen. Do not forget, of course, that you can use it on wood as well.

Liquid Poly This is still a polystyrene cement, but it is very thin and normally comes in a bottle. You apply it with a brush. It is possible to hold the two pieces to be joined together and allow capillery action to take the glue along the join. It can be used on standard plastic kits, but frankly I find it does not really give a reliable join. However, it comes into its own when using plastic card, either on vac forms or scratchbuilds and conversions.

A.B.S. One type such as Micro Weld is formulated for harder Styrenes like Plastruct use. Take great care here to work in a well ventilated room as this can be dangerous if misused.

Solder I mention solder as a type of adhesive, especially for metal models. Frankly, it is not a process which I use myself. It entails using a hot iron with a low melting solder to join the parts. The process requires both care and practice. With the cost of metal kits today you do not especially want to spoil them. I have seen it used very effectively and I know that Ken Jones, Editor of 'Military Modelling' does favour the technique. I would, therefore, refer you to his earlier book in this series (*Guide to Military Modelling*) where he tells you how to do it. Also, there are the actual product manufacturers who will often help. An excellent range of specialist solders, irons and fluxes (an agent to help the solder flow across the part) are produced for modellers by Carrs Modelling Products in the UK. They produce a small booklet which not only tells you how to solder, but explains all the different types of product available and how and when they should be used.

Other tools

There are tools which are nice to have but are not essential.

Needle files are fine files in a variety of shapes such as round, square, oval, flat and triangular plus others. A set of these is not expensive and I find myself using them fairly often. If they become clogged, clean with a wire brush. They are equally useful on a variety of materials, plastic, resin or metal.

A set of jewellers' screwdrivers is often useful, as there are a number of models on the market that require a fine screwdriver for assembly. I canot say I use mine very often, but it is nice to have the right tool for the job when it is required.

If you want to scratchbuild or convert kits, then plastic card is what you need. Usually white, it can be obtained either plain or ready embossed. Transparent card is also available. Plain card can be found in a great variety of thicknesses from 5 thou (5 thousandths of an inch), or 10, 20, 30, 40, 60 and 80 thou. While all have their own uses, 20 thou is perhaps the most used of all. As well as the basic sheets of card, you can also buy Microstrip, which is just evenly sliced strips of card. To try to cut them yourself often leaves you with a warped strip, even if you do manage to keep the width even. This is also available in varying thicknesses.

In addition to the plain card there is a variety of embossed cards available as well. These include some to represent wood planks, corrugated iron sheeting, bricks, tiles, stonework, all in varying styles and patterns. These combine well with the construction accessories from Plastruct, who do tubes, ladders, girders and angle-ions, among others.

To cut out the card, draw on the required shape and score the lines with a sharp knife, using the edge of a steel ruler. Then carefully snap the excess plastic away. That way you will not distort the part as you can by cutting right through in the first place.

If you want to cut circles, then a basic protractor out of a geometry set will score a line just as well.

Card is very versatile. You can laminate different thicknesses to achieve what you want, and then file, sand or carve to shape. You can also bend it to form mudguards etc. by wrapping it around a piece of dowel of the required diameter, immerse it in hot water for a short time, then under cold water to fix it in shape. One way and another, plastic card is one of the AFV modeller's basic raw materials.

The next most useful product to keep around the place is a two-part modelling compound. In the UK it is best known as Milliput and in the USA as the A & B Model Compound. Like epoxy adhesive, this comes in two parts, one of which is a hardener and which has to be mixed well, in equal quantities. It is of a consistency similar to Plasticine, and while it can be carved and sculpted in the same way, it also sets rock hard at the end. It is very popular with modellers who make their own figures, but AFV modellers can also find it useful. Simplest example perhaps would be a complex curved turret in 1/76, such as a Staghound. Build a basic skeleton in card using scale drawings, then fill it up with your Milliput or whatever, keeping it to the basic shape, checking it continually against the drawings, before filing, drilling and adding the required details.

Stretched sprue can be extremely useful for the scratchbuilder. This provides lengths of wire or rod, depending on what you want, with almost infinite variety. It is another use for the handy candle I mentioned earlier. (It still needs to be firmly anchored.) Take a piece of sprue from an old kit and hold it just above the flame. Roll it gently between your fingers to ensure an even spread of heat; then, when it softens, pull from both ends, which will give you even lengths for aerials, bolts or whatever use you may have for it. Tamiya often illustrate the technique on their instruction leaflets to make radio antennae. Larger diameter rods and tubes are commecially available, either in styrene or in brass.

Whatever you are doing, you often need to clamp pieces together while they set. The simplest way is to use sticky tape. I use a masking tape as it is easier and the adhesive tends not to leave marks that need cleaning off. Very basic but effective. An alternative is to use small 'G'-clamps which are obtainable in many hobby and hardware stores.

Another tool along similar lines is known as a 'Helping Hand'. On a base which you fix firmly to the work surface, this consists of one, two or more small clips on multi-jointed arms that you can position to hold a model or a piece of a model at any angle, leaving both your hands free to work on it, either with paints or tools. Finally, there is one other tool which I would classify as a luxury. This is a Pyrogravure. This is basically a heated engraving tool for use on plastic. Figure modellers use it to improve simulated textures – hair, fur and suchlike. The common use for armour modellers is in recreating the Zimmeritt coatings seen on German tanks during the last war. But this is an expensive way of doing it, especially as there are alternatives. One is simply a candle-heated screwdriver. However, more recently there are Zimmeritt punches available from Cesare Gambari in Rome, which can be used on a thin coating of plaster put over the vehicle, very much in prototype manner. The second has recently been released by Promod Accessories, and is a sheet of ready patterned Zimmeritt moulded in a thin sheet of the polyurethene resin, which you simply cut to shape. Yet another imaginative use for this material.

Home Moulding

Can I say first of all, that to copy a complete kit, especially from our smaller manufacturers, must *not* be done. Not only is it against the law of copyright, but it is also morally wrong. These cottage industries survive through us, and indeed they are modellers who have simply decided to share their skills with us. To copy their products would reduce their already limited sales to a point where they are forced to stop, and we would all lose out if no new models are released.

On the other hand, if you want to do a conversion or scratchbuild that requires some extra wheels, then I do not think that any company would object to you making an extra couple of copies of, for example, a particular pattern wheel.

Our first job therefore is to make a mould. This is one way – you can find others. To start with you need a moulding rubber. These should be 'cold-cure' rubbers as they do not require any specialist handling and the chemical reaction as it hardens around the master does not generate heat that will damage it. There are a number of slightly different types, and which one you choose depends on what you want to use it for. If in doubt, ask the dealer. In the UK Alec Tiranti's have been supplying the hobby trade for years. Not only do they produce explanatory booklets but, if you ask them, they will try and help you find an answer to your problem if they can. Having said that, please keep any enquiries relatively short, as obviously they do not have the time to answer very long and complicated questions. Also please try and remember a stamped, self addressed envelope with enquiries.

The instructions which follow are for moulding a simple piece, such as a wheel. Larger and more complicated pieces can be done but they present many problems which are beyond the scope of this guide.

Before you start, read the manufacturer's instructions carefully. Ensure the room is well ventilated. You must also ensure that any chemicals are stored away from children and animals.

A useful accessory is a selection of Lego bricks. These make an excellent moulding box, with straight and secure sides. Fill this box to about a third high with plasticine. Bed the wheel or whatever half into the plasticine. Then pour the mixed rubber compound gently over the part, being careful not to allow any air-bubbles to creep in. Fill the box up, giving about ½ inch of rubber around the part. Let it set. Then turn it over and remove the plasticine. Cut one or two odd key shapes into the excess rubber, to provide locating points when you join the mould for use. Apply a thin coat of vaseline so the two halves don't permanently join. Leaving the wheel in the first half of the mould, pour the rubber to make the second part of the mould. Let it set.

When dry, remove the Lego walls, and there you have the mould. Open it up and remove the original wheel. Then using a sharp knife, cut two feed holes between the wheel and the edge of the mould. One will be the hole to pour the resin in, the other is to let the air out.

To use the mould, tape the two halves together, using two small pieces of board to add support. You then pour the mixed resin into the mould and allow it to set. When it's dry, open the mould and remove your new wheel. Clean it up as necesary, brush out the mould and you're ready to start again.

There are two things to add. Air bubbles leave holes in the castings. One way to get rid of most of these is to brush on a coating of the resin inside the mould before you mix it together. Secondly, for simple items where you don't need detail all round, you can fix it to the base of the mould box and pour the rubber over it. When it's set and you take the master out, you will have an open top mould ready for use. These are obviously the simplest to produce and use.

As far as materials go, you have some choices. The most popular moulding rubbers are probably RTV-11 and RTV-30.

For casting resins, you can now obtain modellers' packs of the polyurethene resin. While the end product is better, the problems tend to be a shorter mould life, a short pot-life (i.e. after mixing you use it immediately or it dries in the mixing pot) and that the mixing of the resin produces small amounts of cyanide, which means you must take safety precautions in line with the manufacturer's instructions. There are alternatives in polyester resins but these smell a lot more and still involve chemicals that you must treat carefully. Do ensure you wear some disposable plastic gloves while working with these.

Those are just the basic principles. There is plenty of choice in moulding rubbers and casting resins, or even low-melt alloys. Look around and try them out; use the ones you feel give the best results.

While we are talking of tools and techniques, something else is a must for any serious modeller – a spares box. Whether you are making straight models or building dioramas, then a spares box is essential. It can take many forms. Mine now occupies four metal drawer cabinets, and needs a fifth. Depending on the size, these can cost anything from £5 to £15. In mine I have a large assortment of wheels, guns, boxes, figures, chassis, body parts, decals, etc. and in a variety of scales. Most models today have optional parts or decals in one form or another, and the secret is to never throw anything away. You never know when they may come in useful. If a model is ever badly damaged, I always salvage wheels, gun-barrels and the like.

5 METAL AND RESIN MODELS

Kit Construction, Conversions and Scratchbuilding

Let's start by going through the assembly of a basic plastic kit.

For our example we will use the *Fujimi Panzer 38t.* Having got the kit, resist the temptation to open the box until you get home.This saves the grief of losing vital parts that fall out on the bus, or wherever. So, get it home, then open it up, and go over the sprues to ensure that all the parts are there, and that none of the mouldings are malformed. This is quite rare but it does happen. The basic tools required are a pair of scissors, to cut parts from the sprue; a craft knife to trim flash and moulding marks; and a tube of glue or a bottle of liquid cement. If there is a choice of variants involving alternative parts, then this is the time to choose which one you want to model.

Go through the instruction sheet and make sure you understand it. Most use symbols to accompany assembly sketches these days, and need to be checked to ensure you do not put glue in the wrong places. The assembly diagrams also indicate which way round many smaller pieces should be fitted. If you are not sure, get hold of some reference photos or plans of the real thing which usually clarify the issue. Then you can begin construction.

The next thing is to follow the construction sequence laid out in the instructions leaflet. This will ensure you don't get to a point and find pieces won't go together because you have already assembled another part which stops you. It is very easy to lose patience and do things in the wrong order just because it takes your fancy.

Some people like to paint parts, such as running gear, prior to assembly, or even before removing the parts from the sprue. I do not agree with this, as the paint can too easily be damaged by sweaty fingers, stray glue, a knife slip, or even through parts not fitting properly. So my preference is to construct things completely

The basic Fujimi 38t kit along with the finished article.

before painting, unless there is interior detail which will be seen and does need to be painted during construction because it would be inaccessible afterwards. Other than that, however, I am a believer in what the eye cannot see the heart will not grieve over.

So, find the first step, which in this case deals with the basic hull and running gear. Identify all the parts you need, and remove them from the sprue onto your working surface, ensuring you can identify each piece. It is easiest to think of them in even smaller sections. Here, for example, you can start with the hull panels. Once you have the separate pieces, trim them with the craft knife to remove any flash or any trace of the joint from the sprue. Then before applying glue, just dry-fit the pieces together to make sure you are getting a good fit of parts. Then apply the glue and fit them together. Next get the suspension units, trim them up as necessary and fit. Finally, do the same for the road wheels, return rollers, rear idlers and drive sprockets. If you have a kit with the flexible track, as we have here, always leave the running gear to set for at least 24 hours. I know they seem solid long before that, but they're not really and, if the track is tight, it will pull them out of shape. The one deviation from the instructions is not to fit the track next, but to leave it until everything is made and painted. The only possible problem with some kits here is that side track guards will often enclose part of the track run, such as on the Churchill Tank, or Matchbox Sherman. With the 38t this is no problem.

Stage 2 involves the fitting of the top track guards and hull details, which is quite straightforward.

Stage 3 is construction of the turret, which moves onto stage 4, where you fit the turret plus stowage accessories to the main hull. So now you should have a fully assembled kit, minus the tracks.

Again give at least twenty-four hours for it to fully set. Then you can paint the basic colour scheme of your choice which, in this case, will be Panzer Grey. I normally get a good coverage with one brush applied coat of Humbrol enamel, provided the paint is fully stirred before use. Then move on and paint the black tyre rims on the main roadwheels. Again, some people use a dark grey as rubber doesn't look black in real life. Well, again, I do not agree as it never looks right to me, whereas matt black is lightened simply by natural light, like the real thing. Tow howsers and tools can then be painted with brown wood, gun metal and/or steel parts. Incidentally, if you want to fit a commander figure, leave it separate for painting and fix in place at the end.

Meanwhile, paint the tracks, where the system depends on the colour plastic involved. Start by painting (if necessary) to overall gun-metal. Then heavily dry-brush with a red-brown/rust colour. Now fit the tracks to the kit, before weathering.

Pick the transfers you want, trim them up, and fit them to the model. Now you have a fully assembled and marked kit, but still rather pristine.

My preferred weathering, particularly for the early Western European campaign, is a dry-brushing with either a tan or dark earth colour. This should be applied to all parts of the model, especially around the bottom hull and running gear. Different shades can indicate dried, damp or wet mud. Finally, lightly dry brush a bright steel over the outside of the track and the teeth of the drive sprockets. You now have your finished model. One of the various systems for fixing decals involves the use of glass or matt varnishes. I do not like these because I find matt varnish unreliable and it can alter the appearance of the painted colours.

Now let us tackle a simple conversion: this time we shall use as a basis one of the 1/76 polyurethene resin kits from Cromwell Models. You can either tackle a conversion outlined in a modelling magazine or pick one for yourself. For this exercise we will choose one of our own.

So you need a scale plan, a selection of which are available from a number of people, as listed at the back of this book. Here I would like to thank Geoff Lacey for providing the drawing for the Horsch Kfz 69 and 20mm Flak mounting, which I had as a basis, even though I chose to use a different gun. Then you need to gather the basic components required, in this case the Cromwell

Same vehicle mounting a Flak 30 used by 'Afrika Korps'

ready ammunition box not
always fitted

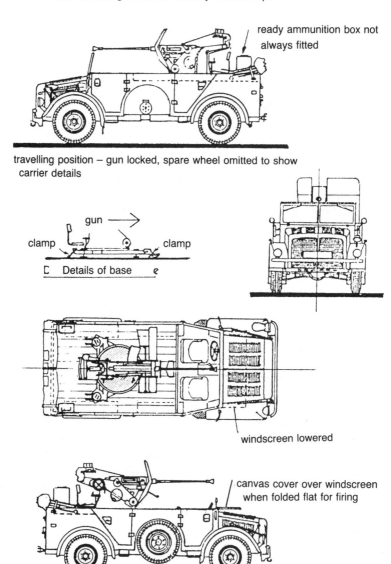

travelling position – gun locked, spare wheel omitted to show
carrier details

gun ⟶

clamp   clamp

Details of base

windscreen lowered

canvas cover over windscreen
when folded flat for firing

firing position – gun released

AUTO UNION/HORCH 1a 4 x 4 Kfz 69 MOUNTING A
FLAK 38 (Erika)
Scale:- 4 m.m. to 1′·0″

Finished in Panzer Grey, and as yet unmarked, the Horsch Flak conversion.

Horsch Kfz 69, the Nitto 20mm Flak 38, and some plasticard. If you wish to do this conversion in 1/72nd scale, then Alby Models in France also produce a fine Horsch.

The Cromwell Horsch has a solid section at the rear and you need to hollow this out slightly to a depth of 2mm, taking care not to damage the exterior body panels. Then fit a rectangular floor over the rear load area, from the bulkhead behind the driver to the rear of the vehicle. The base of the Flak gun needs a little trimming to fit at the two edges, but should be positioned as in the drawings. I know the gun I have used is not that on the drawing, but photos show that both types have been used. They also show that the rolled canvas tilt remained fitted so, to include that, you will need to cut away the load items that are in Cromwell's moulding, taking special care not to damage the tilt-hoop arms at each side.

That is essentially it; it is now ready for painting. The vehicle saw service with the Herman Goering Division both in North Africa and Europe so a variety of colour schemes are possible. Reference photos appear in the 'Encyclopedia of German Tanks', and the markings for the Herman Goering units are in 'Panzer Colours 3', both from Arms & Armour Press.

If you want to convert a standard plastic kit, then the procedure is essentially the same. When converting an AFV, it is common to use just the lower hull and running gear and add a new superstructure from Plasticard. For example, when Airfix first produced their Panzer IV, the first thought was 'ah, at last a Mark IV', and that was accompanied by, 'and what else can I make from it?'. The answers soon followed, and I still have a Jagdpanzer IV, Stug IV, Hummel, PzIVJ and PzIVD which I made at that time.

Another moral is always to keep any unused parts as they may

Camouflage Overall – army mid green. Stars, cross, and side panels – white Panel outlines, and lettering – black. Cross plinth – polished matt teak interior (when seen) veneered mahogany

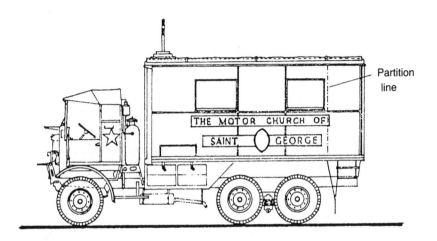

Partition line

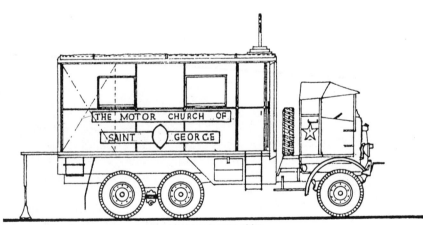

Ready for service doors folded back onto sides

MOBILE CHURCH (CHURCH of ENGLAND)
MOUNTED ON A LEYLAND RETRIEVER CHASSIS
Scale:- 4 m.m. to 1′·0″

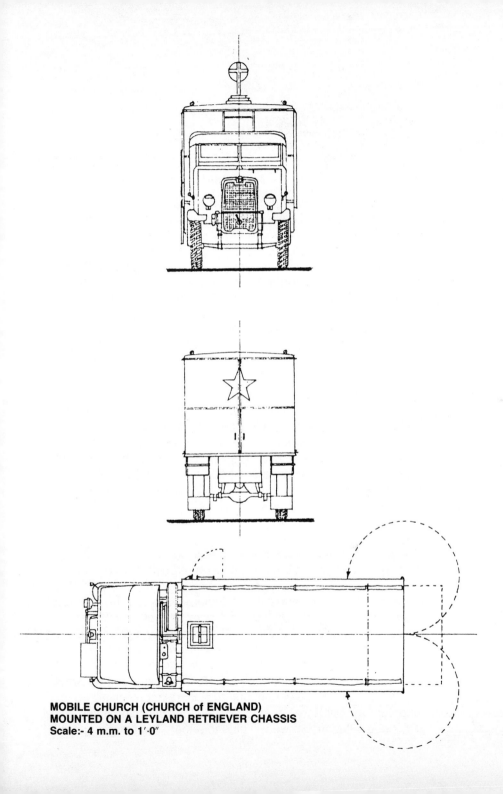

**MOBILE CHURCH (CHURCH of ENGLAND)
MOUNTED ON A LEYLAND RETRIEVER CHASSIS**
Scale:- 4 m.m. to 1'·0"

One of the author's older conversions, a Jagdpanzer IV, built on the Airfix Panzer IV chassis.

come in useful for a later project. You should also be aware of the possibility of using different parts from different kits to get the desired end result.

To let you practise, you will find in this book some scale drawings which you can try your hand at. The mobile Church enables you to convert the Leyland Retriever in Matchbox's 'Monty's Caravan' set, while PzIII SiG 33 requires lengthening the chassis and adding an extra road wheel each side. A good kit to base this on is that from Mathbox, being very reasonably priced. The other two drawings, of the 1/87 Bedford Fire Truck and 1/76 Mack Caravan are included as possible scratchbuilding projects, a subject we will look at shortly.

But before we go on to that, there are other kits available. These are in white metal or resin or indeed sometimes a mixture of both.

Metal models are not new. I have omitted from this book all those ready made models in, normally, 1/43rd scale from Dinky, Corgi, Solido and the like. I am simply considering kits for assembly and finishing by the modeller. In the large scales there are one or two vehicles such as Scale Links Rolls Royce and Bartons Schimitar, but most items are artillery pieces. The real problems associated with anything larger than artillery are cost and assembly.

Due both to the basic cost of metal and also to the cost of making vulcanised rubber production moulds, larger models become so potentially expensive that they would not sell in enough numbers to make the original investment in time and costs worthwhile. The second problem is that, the larger the model, the heavier it becomes. All this extra weight, therefore, means that construction must be handled with care.

Let us look at this by going through the construction of one of Hinchliffe's 1/2 guns, a German Lfh 18. One method of construction would be by soldering but this is rather specialised so, whereas we will look at it again when discussing tools and techniques, this model we will glue together. The first thing to do

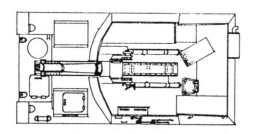

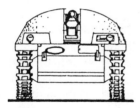 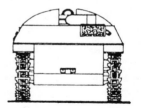

150mm on SIG PzKwII.
1:76 Scale.
7th April 1982
by Trev Claringbold.

Here are two reference shots of the Lfh 18 in the Budge collection, for those of you attempting the Hinchliffe model. Note missing trail spades.

when you get the model is to check carefully that all the parts are there. Then read through the instructions and make sure you understand everything before you start.

Next thing to do, before you assemble anything, is to look carefully over every part and clean off any flash or moulding marks with a sharp modelling knife or a file. Bear in mind that every part will have a moulding mark somewhere, where the metal is fed into the mould. At this time, I would suggest you go through any reference photos you have of the real thing, as it always helps to know exactly what the pieces are supposed to look like and therefore you will recognise if an assembly looks wrong. So I look to assemble various sub-units, paint anything I will not be able to get at later, and then put the whole thing together prior to painting.

I chose to use two different adhesives for this job. I use Devcon 5-minute or Humbrol 2-part epoxy adhesive for the largest and heaviest parts and a Cyanoacrylate, Super Glue 'Extra' for the finer parts. The problems with the epoxy is that you must mix it in small amounts, or it dries before you can use it, and yet it does provide a far stronger joint. Therefore, I use this for the heavier parts, such as the trail arms, while I use the Superglue for the smaller parts which would be difficult to hold in place for a long period of time while the glue dries. I find the thicker Superglue Extra gives better results than the usual thinner one. Now down to work on the gun.

The major parts are showing their age and require quite a lot of cleaning up. In particular, you need to clean away carefully the inside of the slide that is half way down the barrel (Part 6) to get a good fit on the actual recoil slide (Part 5). Throughout the assembly of this kit, and indeed of any other model, continually dry-fit the parts (that is, hold them in place to check the fit but without putting any glue on) to make sure everything is right before you commit yourself to glueing them together. I found that virtually all parts needed a little work, but the gun barrel, trail arms and cradle most of all.

Then simply follow the instructions, which are quite clear. The one thing I did have to do was to re-drill the holes in the gun cradle to take the long screw that mounts the barrel assembly.

I used epoxy glue for the major parts such as mounting the wheels, trail arms, gun shield and recoil spades. All the remaining small parts were fixed with the Cyanoacrylate. I assembled mine in the towing position ready to add to a towing vehicle, but you can have it in the firing position as an alternative.

After allowing a couple of days for everything to set firmly, the gun needs to be undercoated. This can be done either by hand or spray can, in matt white or a matt grey primer. Allow this a good twenty-four hours to dry, and then paint in whatever scheme you require. We will come back to the subject of paints and colours later.

So there you have it. A metal model doesn't have to be complicated; you just have to take it carefully and be aware of different things that may cause you problems.

For those of you with small scale metal models, then these same basic rules apply. Here, in particular, it can be difficult to use solder for anything but the main components such as tracks, hulls and wheels. Any fine parts can be melted by the heat of the soldering iron. So learning to use solder *can* cost you a lot in ruined model parts unless you are very careful. It is largely for that reason that I stick with the different glues.

Resin

There are two types of resin models. The first resin AFV models, back in the early seventies, were made in a polyester resin. This suffered from a number of drawbacks. Firstly, the drying time means production rates are rather slow and, secondly, the resin is hard and brittle, which makes it difficult to mould reliably some fine detail. On top of that, in wargames usage, and even in basic assembly, it shatters if it gets dropped and parts are easily broken off. As a result, the number of people buying resin models during the seventies and early eighties remained relatively small. On the whole, you were expected to provide your own gun barrels and, occasionally, other parts as well. What people really wanted was what one might call a 'complete kit'.

Whilst it is fair to say that Britain has been the real power behind resin models, it was a French maker who began to change things around. Alain Laffargue began producing some superbly detailed kits in what was first referred to as plastic. Infact it was poly-urethene resin. Then towards the end of 1985, Gordon Brown started Cromwell Models, producing a Merkava in the same polyurethene resin. Since then, both Cromwell Models and the polyurethene resin have gone from strength to strength. Other modellers, such as Francois Verlinden in Belgium, have begun to realise the potential of this 'new' material.

It sets solid but is soft enough to be carved with a modelling knife; it successfully moulds even the finest detail, and it glues together well and doesn't shrink as it dries. It dries much quicker than polyester, so speeding production. Models can include gun barrels and machine guns which make them very much complete kits, they don't suffer half as much in the post (don't tell the postman, or he'll try harder!) and don't shatter if you drop them. You can break them but, rather than having a jigsaw puzzle of shattered pieces, they normally have a clean break that you simply glue back together.

The sheer volume of resin models, conversion parts and accessories that have come on the market over the last few years is a testament to the qualities of this new resin, and a sign that the hobby is still healthy and is prepared to buy what it wants. Consider even that early Merkava from Cromwell. When it was released it created a whole new set of standards. Yet now, three years later, it has been upgraded with extra details that include a full set of detailed m.g.'s to mount atop the turret, as manufac-turers realise the vast increase in possibilities that have been opened up. And, most of all, the modeller has not only accepted the resin model but is crying out for more and buying almost everything that can be found.

In 'Small Scale Scene', my monthly column in 'Military Model-ling' magazine, I often deal with 1/76 and 1/72 scale resin models, where I try and keep readers up to date with the latest releases from around the world. A good number of these models are illustrated in this book so, for assembly of a resin model, I will now look at Accurate Armours BMP I in 1/35th scale.

The prices are higher than a conventional plastic kit, but they seem to be falling into a band of prices around £30 in the UK and $60.00 in the USA. It does vary according to the size and complexity of the model, but this is currently about average.

The BMPI came in a sturdy cardboard box, well packed with polystyrene foam chips. So, first of all, it had not suffered from postal handling. Packaging is extremely important when you order mail order from what can sometimes be the other side of the world. Included are a good set of instructions and assembly hints as well as a background history of the real vehicle.

Again, you must go over all the parts to remove any fine flash and clean up any moulding marks. I found very little work was needed. As with the metal gun, it still helps to check the fit of parts with a dry-run. I found that the long piece with track guard and suspension arms on one side had become warped.

To correct it, simply immerse the part in hot water and, as it softens in the warmth, gently bend it back to correct shape. Run it under cold water and it will be correctly 'fixed'. Then proceed with assembly.

For polyurethene resin, I use just a cyanoacrylate glue, as I find it works very well. You can use the polystyrene cement used for conventional kit assembly but, while it does hold things together, it doesn't bond them properly. Nothing is worse than a slight knock and your latest pride and joy falling apart.

If any parts don't fit cleanly, and I have to say they all did on the BMP, then identify where it isn't fitting and gently scrape or trim the offending obstruction with a sharp craft knife. Keep stopping to check for fit until you get it right.

Once the model is assembled, give it a gentle wash with soapy water to take off any residues from the moulding process and then it is almost ready to be painted. You can use an undercoat or simply take a look at every part of the model. Look for any holes in the mouldings that have been left by air bubbles in the resin. These should be filled with Miliput (A & B Modelling Compound in the USA) or some other filler, and sanded or filed smooth. You can do this before assembly, but I do it afterwards as one can spend time on parts that will never be seen anyway and I'm too lazy to do

Painted but not weathered, Accurate Armour's BMPI.

things that aren't necessary. Let the model dry, then paint, using whatever type of paints you prefer.

Most resin models tend to consist of a relatively few number of parts, yet look most effective. The BMP has a one-piece hull, but has separate road wheels and short lengths of trackwork to fix around them. I enjoyed making this one and the finished item was very pleasing, as was the knowledge that there are far less of these about than, say, a Tamiya T62. I look forward to trying another of Accurate Armours models before much longer.

Then there are those models that mix the materials used in the kit. An excellent example of this for our purposes is featured on the cover of this book. Miltra produce a brace of 1/35 model Russian T80's. One is the basic tank, while the second includes a full array of reactive armour. The T80 is still the subject of a great deal of speculation, so it is very difficult to say how accurate this is. However, Miltra drew up a set of plans which were circulated to as many checkers they could find to get corrections. Indeed, despite the models being at an advanced stage, one of these corrections necessitated a complete remake of the tracks. Bearing that in mind, and with no more definite unclassified sources to check, it is certainly full of interest. The model consists of resin mouldings for the turret, hull, roadwheels, side skirts, fuel drums, snorkel and box, and stowage. The other details, such as main gun barrel, AAMG, smoke discharges, ammunition boxes, trackwork and some reactive armour sections, are in metal. Both the resin and the metal parts needed a fair bit of cleaning up prior to assembly and a number of the turret fittings need to have location holes drilled for them. Fortunately, the accompanying drawings and instructions are a good guide. I found it essential to keep dry-fitting the parts to check them during the cleaning up process.

The trackwork is cast in shorter white metal lengths that run from the drive sprocket to idler, without any top run which would be hidden by the side skirts anyway.

I fully assembled mine before supplying any paintwork. I find this means a better bond for the glues where no paint interferes. Then, with the model fully assembled, you have a mixture of the two different materials. Now, if you want a decent paint coverage, you need to cover the bright silver metal and dull resin with a uniform colour. So undercoat the model with matt white or grey. Then put your camouflage colour on. One of the best colour matches for modern Soviet armour, I am told, is Humbrol Matt 30,

Dark Green. Then apply dark washes and dry-brushing to weather the vehicle and, in turn, highlight the details. If you have the reactive armour kit, some major blocks are moulded on to the turret roof and hull glacis plate. I used neat matt black to emphasise the joins between the separate explosive blocks (reactive armour consists of individual blocks of explosive, which are detonated when hit by a shell or missile and the outward explosion counteracts the incoming force of the shell; the two opposing forces cancel each other out and therefore stop anything piercing the basic vehicle armour).

Vac Forms

I cannot leave construction methods without mentioning vac-forms made, as the name suggests, by using vacuum suction to pull a heated sheet of plastic down over a mould. This is not a particularly widespread technique in the AFV modelling field, unlike the model aircraft world. I have mentioned the various manufacturers in previous sections. I won't claim to being an expert on these techniques, as frankly I am not overstruck on the quality of the finished article, and the amount of time and effort involved does not compare with what can be accomplished with resin models. However, they do exist and it is perhaps rather unfair to pass my prejudices on.

The basic parts come on plastic sheets. You cut out each part, trimming close around it. Then you need a flat surface: a sheet of glass is ideal. Tape down some wet and dry paper and sand the piece keeping the pressure even all round. Eventually you will find the excess rim of plastic comes away leaving the part you require. The fit of these parts is seldom ideal and you do need to keep checking against a set of scale drawings. A fair amount of filler is always required as is sanding down afterwards.

When assembling vac-formed parts, use a liquid polystyrene cement. If there are some white metal parts, then I find a cyanoacrylate glue best. There are one or two kits of interest to justify the time, but the rapid expansion of resin models is quickly leaving them behind.

Scratchbuilding

The art of scratchbuilding has, I believe, waned a little in recent years, except among the real enthusiasts. In my opinion, the

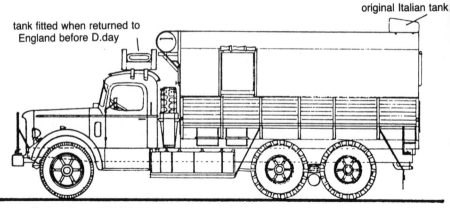

original Italian tank

tank fitted when returned to England before D.day

Bodywork as with eighth army

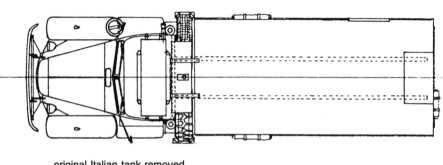

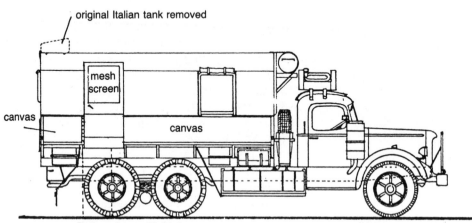

original Italian tank removed

canvas

mesh screen

canvas

Bodywork as with 21st. army group

**FIELD MARSHAL B.L. MONTGOMERY'S
MOTORISED CARAVAN MOUNTED ON A MACK NR4 CHASSIS**
Scale:- 4 m.m. to 1'·0"
**March 1977
Sheet 1**

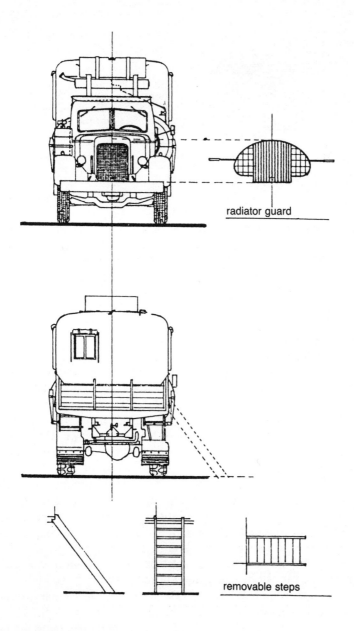

radiator guard

removable steps

FIELD MARSHAL B.L. MONTGOMERY'S
MOTORISED CARAVAN MOUNTED ON A MACK NR4 CHASSIS
Scale:- 4 m.m. to 1′·0″
March 1977
Sheet 1

This Krupp 6x6 was one of the author's earlier scratchbuilds. All in plasticard it only uses wheels from the Airfix 88mm carriage.

reason for this has been the more widespread acceptability of resin models among the modelling and wargaming public. Combined with the huge variety of subjects that are still coming onto the market on a regular basis, there is simply a decreased need to scratchbuild for yourself. Nevertheless, it provides you with an opportunity to be creative and to display your own modelling skills which, however good or bad, can lead to something that will provide a good deal of self-satisfaction.

Here I don't want to get an individual example as there are suitable scale drawings included in this book and available from a variety of other sources for you to try. It is odds on that your earliest attempts will leave something to be desired, but don't let that put you off. It takes time, practice and patience. I still have my earliest efforts. They're not brilliant, but they mean a lot to me.

Having chosen your subject and scale, you will need to gather the required materials together. You must start with a scale drawing. I recommend that having obtained them, get a copy to use as a working drawing. Suppliers will not object to you doing this provided it is purely for your own working purposes only. Then you will need a selection of different thickness plasticards. The most useful are 10, 20 and 40 thou. sizes, while others come in handy from time to time. There may also be some accessory parts which you can use from your spares box. Probably the most likely are wheels. If I have spares or a broken model I always keep the wheels, as these are very awkward to make from scratch.

So, armed with your tool box, you can start cutting plastic. Having drawn out, traced, or marked the required shape on to the card, use a very sharp craft knife to score carefully round the part. Then simply bend it round the scoring to snap out the part. To try to cut right through, especially with scissors, can end up warping the part. There is also another important point to consider here. Do not forget to allow for the width of the card involved in any joint while cutting out the card. To simplify this point, consider this next example.

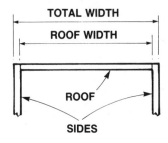

In this example, the width of the roof you need will not be the actual width shown on the drawings.

If you buy a kit the instructions are broken down into sub-assemblies. The same applies here. Decide on the assemblies you can use, e.g. cab, chassis and body *or* hull, turret, running gear and accessories. Any large assembly, such as hull or large truck body, will benefit from including some bulkheads inside. These will keep everything square (provided you cut them right) and add strength to the finished model. After the main hull or body comes the sub-assemblies that fit on and around it, such as mudguards, fuel drums, turrets, wheels and running gear.

You will need curved mudguards, particularly in wheeled vehicles. Cut the correct shape from flat card and find a piece of dowel of the required diameter. Wrap the card round the dowel and immerse in hot water, then into cold water, which will fix the card in shape. Remove from the dowel and trim to get a correct shape and fit before fixing to the model.

Another major sub-assembly is often a turret. Sometimes these are made up from nice flat panels, but not always. You may have a more complex shape such as the Staghound MkI turret for example. These can be built up in two ways.

One is to use flat pieces of card cut roughly to shape, but oversize, and built up to the height of the required turret. Using something such as protractors to check your work against scale drawings, sand or file the rough shape down to match the drawings.

(not to scale)

The second way is to use the drawings to get the right size and shape for a basic framework, which you can then fill in with something such as Miliput and then file to shape. Use a turret ring, cross section and profile as your frame.

 OR (not to scale)

You then have all the details to add, which can be made from card, sprue, rod scrap plastic or spare parts. Applied with care, these can add that special finishing touch. To get them right, it is best always to have as many photographic references on hand as you can manage, to support the scale drawings.

Designed to be used for large scale models, but sometimes useful for smaller ones as well, are the rivets, nuts and bolts and similar fittings available from Grandt-Line in the USA, obtainable in the UK from both E D Models and Historex Agents.

There are two other methods of simulating rivets, especially for smaller scale modellers. The first requires practice. Mark to rivet positions on the *rear* of the card part prior to assembly, and using something such as a compass point, press from the inside, taking care not to pierce the card. This will produce a rivet 'bump' on the external surface. It does take practice to get a uniform effect, but it works. The second method requires patience. Holding stretched sprue close to a candle flame will cause the tip to melt back in a mushroom (or rivet) shape. Cut off the rivet and repeat the process to give the necessary number for your chosen subject.

This leaves two other points to consider when building with plastic card. The best adhesive to use for assembling plastic card points is a liquid cement and not tube glue. Secondly, the one thing I have omitted is that not all joints will be at 90° angles. So if it is an angled joint, bevel the edges to get a better joint:

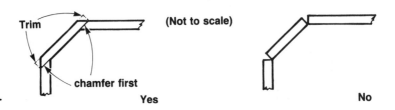

Trim   (Not to scale)

chamfer first

Yes   No

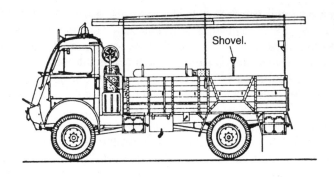

Shovel.

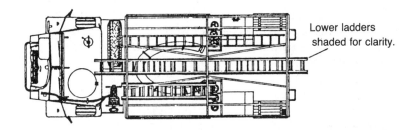

Lower ladders
shaded for clarity.

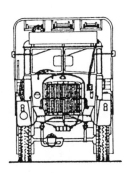
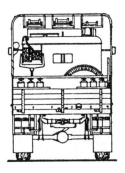

BEDFORD 'QL', Army Fire Service.
1/87 Scale.
20–3–'85
Drawn by Trevor Claringbold

For additional external details, there are many useful accessories now readily available. In particular, there is fine mesh in etched brass which is very useful in the engine deck screening that you frequently find on AFV's or on truck radiators. Also readily available are items such as brass wire and tubing which can make grab handles and gun barrels respectively. Plastic accessories such as Plastruct have round and square cross section pieces, plus girders, ladders and other useful parts. Keep your eyes open for anything that might be used to achieve the desired end result.

In conclusion, I have purposely left out the idea of home vac-forms. I have seen a number of people recently suggesting ways of using home cookers to heat plastic sheet on some home-built frames. The thought of someone making a mistake, or overheating the plastic to cause a fire or serious burn if molten plastic is stuck on their skin, is not worth the risk. There are far safer alternatives as with the case of making a rubber mould from one master that enables you to produce any number of pieces. No doubt some of you out there use the technique successfully, but I do not feel this should be encouraged in less experienced modellers. You can buy proper vac-forming machines but they are expensive and can be difficult to get hold of, and would probably only be used by experienced and dedicated modellers.

6   CREW FIGURES AND ACCESSORIES

Dealing first with 1/87 scale, Minitanks do produce one or two sets of commander figures for both modern and WWII AFVs. In the larger 1/76 scale, there has been an increasing tendency to provide interesting crew figures. Most Airfix vehicles had basic crew figures, but their positions/stances were always rather wooden. Compare, for example, the crew figures in Airfix's SdKfz 7 and those in the Matchbox SdKfz II. With the driver and commander, Airfix provide few identical seated figures. Matchbox give you the driver and then two pieces which mould three figures in a block. Each of the three figures are in a different pose, and when the two blocks are reversed to face each other they don't immediately look the same.

As the manufacturers have gained experience of what the market wants, and quality has improved, so have the figures. There is far more imagination shown today. Examples are the crew figures with ESCI's 25 Iber, and the driver in Matchbox's Diamond T. Likewise, the details of the uniforms are far more recognisable today.

These requirements have also been met by the smaller manufacturers of our resin and metal models. Many of them now make a point of having open hatches on their AFVs and often of providing their own crew figures. Both Red Star and MMS have begun to provide figures for their Soviet vehicles. Cromwell have gone just slightly further, with the variety now in some of their figures. Their French Renault D2 has an interesting figure clambering through the front hull hatch, and their recent German SzKfz 250/9 half-track has a beautifully relaxed figure in the turret. Wearing a soft cap and hooded anorak, he is leaning forward, arms folded, on top of the turret. The anatomy is also good on these figures which always makes me happy to use them. Unfortunately you can still find figures that are anatomically poor and therefore spoil the whole look of a model.

Though not perfect in scale, this Platoon 20 M113 ACAV with crew figures is full of atmosphere for the Vietnam period.

Moving on to 1/35th scale, there are now a huge variety of figures available. The main AFV producer is Tamiya, and they usually include one figure and sometimes more. Just how good they are does vary from one to another, but again I find their basic anatomy to be quite acceptable. They put a good degree of effort into finding something different and do not simply rely on providing a figure in strictly regulation uniform every time.

My first example is that of the commander supplied with their Challenger, who is wearing a winter quilted anorak of British Army issue. This compares with the US special forces crew figure in their new M113 ACAV release, who, armed with a captured AK47, is modelled running from the vehicle, soft hat and all. This, to me, shows some thought as to where the vehicle was really used and just what could be expected to be seen with it. Perhaps my favourite example is the crew supplied with their Panzer IV D. They are dressed in the early black Panzer uniform, complete with berets and, once you have painted and positioned them into a grey but grimy Panzer, they have the air of conquerors riding secure in their own image of invincibility. I have always been able to picture this model driving on a cobbled road past some houses, with civilians, and particularly children, watching them pass by in a kind of stunned shock.

Most especially, though, our resin and metal accessory makers have fastened onto the possibilities. For example, Barton Miniatures do an American tank crew, set in Vietnam, to go with other figures they produce. Then, still in metal, Piper Model Castings produce some nice tank crews, such as modern Soviet, WWII British crews for both late war, Western European and 8th Army figures. These are very highly detailed and come up well with a good paint job. They also produce some nice figures under licence from Jareau figures in Japan. Two that come to mind are one in shirt sleeves and braces, trousers untucked from his boots

Afrika Korps Panzer commander from Verlinden Productions.

Vietnam US tank commander from Velinden Productions.

and another in uniform, leaning on one side with the weight of carrying a full jerry can. Touches like this make for that 'something' which can set a model apart. It is always useful to remember that vehicles may be in combat for 5% of their time, but are out of combat for 95%. Maintenance, refuelling, eating, sleeping or simply waiting is a far more common situation than fighting.

There are other resin manufacturers producing crew figures, such as Des Resin doing French figures and ADV doing British figures in the late war tank suit. Belgo figures, as the name suggests, come from Belgium. This is quite a large range of figures in white metal. While there are some exceptions, by far the bulk cover WWII period. There are both civilian and military figures. The figures are simple in that they are either in one piece, or an occasional arm or leg needs to be fixed on. Despite this simplicity, these figures are really nice. The quality of detail and anatomy are very good. Some of the choices of uniform are equally well thought out and there are a good number of AFV crewmen. An extra sub-range of figures are for the Ardennes fighting in 1944 and there are some evocative US and German soldiers, well wrapped in Greatcoats and fighting the cold as much as the enemy. Another important point in their favour is the very reasonable price range that compare well with other available figures.

However, the leader in this field has got to be Verlinden Productions. The range and quality of both the metal and resin figures they are now producing is of the highest quality.

There are Tank Crew sets, consisting of three $\frac{1}{2}$ or $\frac{1}{4}$ figures, with

Plenty of Verlinden accessories here. For the basic 1/35 Tamiya M8 GMC, there are resin crew figures, ammunition, boxes and packs, plus Normandy farm building.

WWII crews in Russian, American, Afrika Korps and German European uniforms, modern US, Nato and Israeli, plus US Vietnam period figures. Then individual, complete commanders for US WWII, Vietnam and modern; Israeli tank and APC figures; and WWII German European and Afrika Korps. In addition to these and their other figures, they have made available separate sets of different heads. By changing these around, you can use the same figure yet have it look completely different. There are other 'universal' figures whose nationality is indistinguishable. How about combining their sleeping, awakening and washing soldiers which would do well to picture an AFV crew early in the morning, and perhaps one of the resin mechanic figures (which are dressed in a common over-all), who could be beginning to prepare some breakfast!! The potential of the Verlinden range is immense. For those of you needing details of colour schemes for these figures, we will see a little later some of the places to look for them. We cannot really leave Verlinden Products without looking at the rest of their products.

To assist in finishing your vehicles, they have a number of sheets with rub-down dry decals. There are a good variety, covering WWII German, Russian, French and Allied Tank insignia, markings and slogans, as well as others for Israeli vehicles and US vehicles in Vietnam. They are all of good quality and worthwhile obtaining. I have always felt it strange that the armour modeller has so few commercial decal sheets available. The aircraft modeller has hundreds. Other than Verlinden, the Almark decal sheets have been really useful. First produced in the sixties, these water slide decals in 1/76 and some in 1/35 are now available again, produced by E.D. Models in Birmingham. Outside of these, the only others I know of are in 1/87 from Roco for their Minitank range, and Skytrex have recently begun doing basic insignia for their 1/200th range.

So once it has been painted and marked, you begin to add other accessories to get that lived-in look. There is camouflage net, to be draped or rolled as required. Then there are painted card accessories, such as pavement/sidewalks, maps, signs and ration cartons. The ration cartons, in particular, are frequently seen pictured stowed on AFVs. Maybe the tanks have "gotta have gas" but the crews still march on their stomachs.

Next they have turned to yet another material, with some imaginative uses for etched brass. There is a large set of spaced armour for an Israeli M113, a set of .30 and .50 cal ammo belts, WWII German and American webbing; barbed wire, ornamental iron gates and assorted plants. This is probably the best example of a manufacturer who has realised the potential of using different materials for different products, using each to their best advantage.

Most of all, Verlinden has moved heavily into using the new polyurethene resin. One of the main accessories missing from virtually any AFV kit is that of the ammunition. They now have some highly detailed sets in a variety of calibres, each with a variety of shot. There are HEAT, HESH, HE and AT, plus empty cases and ammunition boxes. They range from 37mm up to 155mm. On top of this, there are other sets of small arms and tank ammunition boxes, all of which can make useful stowage on AFV's, or loads from soft-skins during re-munitioning operations. Francois Verlinden first made his name by building dioramas, so it is no surprise that all these products are designed to encourage people into that field.

Other accessories include tank crew gear, bottles and cans, welding gear, radio sets, jerry cans, ruined buildings and oil drums. The detail is excellent and there seems to be no end to their new releases.

However, there are still other accessories available. In the UK, Promods produce a series of accessories in the older polyester resin, as well as items such as lighting sets. These are not really competitive to Verlinden, more complimentary. The boxes and bed rolls are not as precisely detailed, but do well to fill in some background. But there are more particular items, such as a set of furniture which is designed to fit in Verlindens Ruined House Interior on translucent green resin 'puddles' to be set into the groundwork of a diorama. Most interesting are lighting sets. Coloured L.E.D.'s (Light Emitting Diodes) are available, either on or flashing. Colours are red, green and yellow and the diodes can

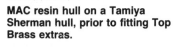

MAC resin hull on a Tamiya Sherman hull, prior to fitting Top Brass extras.

Top Brass accessories ready for using on the MAC Sherman conversion. The Browning .50cal is superb.

be cut and carved to any shape you require. The kits come complete with circuit board and connectors so it can be run off a small batttery.

Promods (which is, incidentally, another range distributed by Tyresmoke Products) also do a small selection of accessories in 1/72 scale. These are aimed primarily at aircraft modellers but are of equal use on AFV's. From the USA are In-Country Hobbies. This is a series of 1/35 accessories for modelling items set in Vietnam. Recently changed over to the polyurethene resin, there are M72 LAW rockets, shotguns, grenades, Claymore mines, hats and Starlite scopes. Best are the "Marmite" ice boxes and kool cans which were so often seen adorning AFVs in S.E. Asia. They tend to need a fair bit of cleaning up, but provide some extremely useful items.

If you want 1/76 and 1/72 accessories, then both Fujimi and ESCI produce some very useful sets, with various tools, boxes, crates and sandbags, all of which provide excellent stowage.

In the past, Airfix did some diorama sets, one set in Europe, one in North Africa and one in the Far East. Each of these contained a useful set of accessories. There were coils of barbed wire, bicycles, picks and shovels, plus various crates. Keep an eye out for these bits and pieces.

Another product of the sixties was the range of Armourtec Accessories from the Bellona Scenary company. These were injection moulded plastic sets of AFV tools, jerrycans and M.G.'s. Again, these sets do turn up occasionally. If you prefer 1/87, then Roco have a set of barrels, crates and tents for use with their range of vehicles, as does Model Transport with crates and jerry cans.

Now, if after all this you still do not find what you want, there are other alternatives. One is you can make your own master, then mould it and cast more in resin. The second alternative is surprisingly often overlooked. The answer can be to look outside the bounds of the Military Modelling hobby. In particular, take a look around the Railway hobby shops. You will often find a variety of useful accessories in a selection of scales. I quite regularly look round one of these specialist shops, and frequently find useful bits or ideas. They need not necessarily be used for what they were originally intended, just be aware of what you might use the various shapes for. Even their farm animals like horses, sheep and cows could well find a place in a diorama. After all, Tamiya have produced just such a set for their 1/35 models. For the major manufacturers, Italeri have some accessory kits, including tools, jerry-cans and modern small-arms.

7 COLOURS AND CAMOUFLAGES

Early British AFV's were painted light grey, a symbol of its background from the Royal Navy's ironclads. Only later did they begin to acquire Multi-coloured camouflage schemes, or appear as plain green. At the same time as AFV's came into use, so we had the growth of not only anti-armour weapons but also air reconnaisance.

There are two essential ingredients to camouflage. One is to hide the vehicle, though that only really works while the vehicle is stationary, and the second is to confuse the shape in the eyes of any observer and thereby throw-off the enemy's aim.

More recently, they have developed thermal camouflage netting which not only works visually, but also hides the heat of the vehicle from infra-red and thermal-imaging detection equipment. As technology defeated camouflage, so we now have to have technical camouflage to deceive that detection equipment. It all adds up to confusion. Unfortunately this confusion flows over into the modelling hobby as well. I do not promise to give any answers, but I hope I might give you a slightly different viewpoint or two.

Over the years, though admittedly more often among aircraft modellers, I have been tired of hearing people argue over just what such and such a colour should be. Let us take one of the most common, the Olive Drab used on US vehicles. Even the various paint manufacturers produce a variety of different shades for this colour. So which do you choose? If you look at restored vehicles you will see that their colours vary. If you look at colour photographs, so the colours vary as does the quality of the film itself. Then again, a new vehicle looks, on the whole, much darker than an older vehicle which has been exposed to the elements for any length of time. On top of all this, different batches of the real paints, even from the same manufacturer, let alone different ones, will not necessarily be exactly the same shade.

The answer for the modeller finally comes down to just what you feel is the best match. The best answer in my opinion is to keep your own set of colour chips. With greens in particular, there is a huge choice. Take a piece of plastic card and paint a sample patch of each colour, along with its identifying pot number. That way, depending upon whatever green you are looking for, you can get a good idea of which one to use before you even start. You can of course do the same with browns, reds, greys or any other colours.

Let us look at the post 1943 scheme of sand/green/red-brown used by the Germans. The overall sand colour was applied at either the point of manufacture or base workshops during major overhauls. Again, the paint was produced by various manufacturers which led to different shades and, as the war progressed badly for Germany, so the quality of the raw materials deteriorated, and the shade of colour would be changed. As for the green and red-brown, these were supplied in cans in a form of paste, to go with the vehicle. In this way the scheme could be varied by the individual units and crews to suit the local surroundings. The paints had to be diluted, either in petrol or water. Just the dilution of those mixtures was variable and therefore the greens could be light or dark, and the brown could appear between light red or dark brown. Water-based mixtures then obviously became affected by heavy rain, driving through rivers or whatever, and therefore rapidly appeared faded and tatty. Yet more variation was introduced by whether the crew brushed it on by hand, or whether it was done by a spray gun driven off a compressor. This would depend on what equipment a unit had available in the field. When you add to that the patches of new paint over repairs or replacement parts, you can understand the huge variation in colours that can occur, and this is largely without the effects of weathering, which we will look at shortly. On that basis, therefore, I do not see how anyone can say a particular shade is right or wrong. Make up your own mind.

There are really three types of paint available to use: enamels, acrylics and oils. So again you are faced with a choice. You can stick to one or the other or use all three. Each have their uses and you need to decide which you prefer and when.

Acrylic paints do have disadvantages. I have found that applying a second coat is nearly always required and it can cause the first coat to come away, leaving an awful finish. I have also heard it reported as 'cracking' after a period of time. All in all I have a number of reservations about acrylic paints, but that does not mean I discount them completely. Their advantage is that brushes can be cleaned in plain water, and if a pot dries out then a drop of water will reconstitute it. One other problem I have found has been with Tamiya acrylics. The colours are all right but they do smell strongly.

Oil paints can be mixed to a huge variety of colours and their long drying time allow you to adjust anything until you are happy with it. For AFVs, however, you will not get a truly matt finish, whatever you add. I have known someone to use oils on 1/76th AFVs, but I cannot claim to have been too happy with the results. Personally, I use oils in two areas, where its semi-gloss property and texture is ideal: For flesh on 1/35th scale figures, it is useful to have the time to blend in all the flesh tones. The second area is for use on modelling horses. The sheen and texture of raw oil paint produces the best results I know.

This leaves us with enamels. There are a number of makes available, with Roco's own brand, Airfix and Revells own brands, and Testors, but by far the largest and most well known must be Humbrol. I have accumulated a host of Humbrol colours over the years, some I use a lot, some I use only very occasionally. Painting AFVs, the greatest variety are the different greens. I hand paint my models as I have never got round to the expense of an airbrush and compressor. I find that I can get a perfectly adequate coverage with just one coat. To use more tends to block and obscure the finer detail. Using spray cans may help make life quicker, but again it is very easy for the paint to run into corners or on to edges and build up to unsightly lumps and bumps. That provides you with the basic vehicle colour. On top of this, you add all the other effects that you want.

The ability to get that coat of paint right first time depends on preparing it correctly. I would never work directly from the paint tin. Whenever I finish a pot of paint or, alternatively if it dries up solid, I always save the lid when I throw away the tin and use the lids as pallets. Stir the paint well (I usually use the handle of a paint brush) and transfer some to the working lid. Provided you have stirred it right in the first place, then this will give the correct matt finish throughout. If you work from the main tin, the paint tends to settle again and as you work from the surface, so it will not dry with the correct matt finish, and you will have to start all over again. You may have a large job to paint. If the lid-full is not enough, never mind, just keep repeating the process. Always remember to re-stir the paint each time.

The only colour which does not give an ideal coverage first time is matt white, which usually takes two or three coats. You can also use matt white to undercoat white metal models. The finish is usually very poor but that does not matter in this case. It has two purposes. Firstly it shows up any faults, problem or details, which you can either correct or pick-out later. Secondly it provides a base for your required colour scheme to be painted on to. You should always allow it twenty-four hours at least before applying the next colour.

You will always need brushes. They vary in size from 000, 00, 0, 1, 2, 3 etc., though these are the main ones to interest us. I do not favour cheap brushes, except for larger brushes which I use to put on main coats for a large model or white undercoats on metal ones. Use better brushes to put on detail or camouflage patterns. You can get 'sable' brushes which are the most expensive, and synthetic brushes at most art shops. I find that these are usually slightly more reasonably priced and just as good as sable. Whichever you buy, look for a brush that gets a good point. These brushes are sold for water colour painting and most good art shops keep a jar of water handy for you to test the brush. When wet it should go to a fine point, without any bristles poking out at odd angles. If there are any odd bristles, do not buy it – you are looking for a fine point. If you go in a hobby shop, look for their more expensive and better brushes, as many of the cheaper ones are no good at all for any decent work.

Always ensure you clean your brushes well after use. You can clean enamels in white spirit turpentine or a branded thinner, and you must always then rinse the brush out in water. I always then dry the brush on an old cloth, which shows if there are any paint traces in the moisture from the brush. If there is any trace, then re-clean the brush. If you look after your brushes it pays dividends and gives them a reasonable life-span. Once the fine point wears down I relegate them to more general use. Next we move on to weathering, that is if you want to. You do have the option of leaving it in a 'factory fresh' condition. Alternatively you can make it look as used as the real thing. My only word of warning is not to go too far. Decide first where and when you want to set your vehicle. The dry dust of the 1940's drive through France will clearly warrant less than the thick, clinging, winter muds of the Eastern Front in 1943. Whatever you choose, too little is always better than too much. My own preference is always for a light coating of dust.

A common first step is to apply a black wash. This is a mixture of around 10% matt black and 90% thinners. Apply with a large soft brush and then use a piece of cloth or sponge to wipe most of it off. This leaves the paint collecting in cavities around the moulded detail and providing a general grime.

A next step can be to add a slightly darker black wash around fuel caps to show staining, and orange/red rust stains. Again understatement is always the best solution – do not get drawn in to over-doing things.

The next step is the opposite technique, that of 'dry-brushing.' Here again you use raw paint from the pallet-lid, using a fairly large brush. Having put paint on the brush, wipe most off on to some newspaper, and then apply the almost dry brush, drawing it over the model. This will leave traces of the paint on any surface, but particularly on sharp edges and details. This same technique is used to highlight the detail. This time mix the basic colour and add a little white. Use the paler colour, but be careful not to make it too white, and again dry-brush it over the details. This accentuates the fine details on a model for the viewer of the finished article. For dried and fresh mud/dust, dry-brush different shades of brown/tan.

When modelling armoured or soft-skin vehicles, you have the option of including signs of both general wear and tear and battle damage. These can feature bent and damaged mudguards, scratches to the bottom front of the hull, gouged armour plate, broken glass or even bullet/shell holes. I have too often seen these effects badly done and over done and my advice is to always understate it, unless you want to model something totally destroyed, in which case you present yourself with new problems. The best way to go about this is to consider just where the vehicle is supposed to be. For example, a desert vehicle is likely to remain reasonably sound compared, say, to an M48 or Centurian in the Vietnam jungle, where track-guards were regularly damaged. Once you have chosen the scene, study as many photographs as you can that relate to your choice, and this will guide you in what to do and what not to do.

If you select to model a destroyed vehicle, again study as many photographs as you can. Some armoured vehicles literally split apart at the seams if ammunition inside explodes. In this case, much internal detail will become visible and will therefore require modelling. Rubber tyres on road wheels will be burnt down to the wheel rims with grey ash remaining. Fire will blacken the vehicles and burnt off paint leaves the metal to rust.

In-action shots such as this M48 in Vietnam are good references for markings and service modifications such as removing the cupola .50cal to the top, giving greater flexibility. Note C-ration cartons behind the mantlet.

For a final effect, instead of paint, use the weathering powders that are available. These can help you blend a model into the groundwork of a diorama. There are one or two alternatives: Carrs Modelling Products have some very fine powders, using oil-based industrial pigments. They can be mixed, blended and also streaked, using diluted detergent which can create some interesting effects. Another alternative is to use ground-up artists pastels. Readily available in art shops, there is a good variety of colours available. Apply them with a soft brush. The only problem is that after application, you must be careful not to touch the model, as it smudges. So only apply this after fixing the model to a base. If you want to handle it, such as on smaller wargame models, then use paint for your weathering, not powders.

I have already mentioned that I am not an air-brush user. There are still one or two ways to produce some interesting effects, using a brush. One is, to use a cut-down brush, using a thinned paint, but with most of the paint wiped off, as if dry-brushing. Apply the camouflage colour with a stipple action. Practice on some scrap plastic to judge the correct application. The second technique takes a little more practice to get it right. Used correctly you can achieve that sprayed-on look. Pick one panel of the vehicle at a time and paint the outline of your required pattern in virtually

This not only gives details of the vehicle and the crews' uniforms and weapons, but also shows how cramped and vulnerable they would be if caught by a mine. These troops of 1st Infantry Division are just north of Saigon in 1965. (US Army).

neat paint and then use pure thinners, while the colour is still wet, to dilute it and fill in between the lines. With experience, this achieves excellent results.

There is a great deal of expense involved in purchasing an air-brush system. You then need an even more expensive compressor. 'Tinned Air' is available but it is not cheap if you use a lot of it, and the pressure varies between an empty and a full can. Then there are many arguments about how you should mix the paint to get the correct consistency for use with the air-brush. If you get it wrong it can produce a colour too thin, or a paint that is so thick it clogs the spray itself. Then, if it is incorrectly mixed it can produce splatters. All of these are excellent ways to really depress yourself. The only real solution is to have plenty of practice.

I therefore think it fair to say that you have to be determined enough to want to use one and be able to afford it. A relatively small number of modellers use them; Most of us get by without them. If you really want to try one, there are a number of books available on air-brushing. On the other hand, get in touch with someone who does use one and who will talk you through their experiences.

Many people use matt varnish to give a final sealing coat to their models. If that suits you, fine, but personally I do not like to. In my opinion it tends to give an unnatural sheen to the model. Many use it in the process of hiding decal carrier film. Trimming round them is my preferred way. Another problem is, that if you do not mix the matt varnish correctly, then it simply will not dry matt, and may leave a white deposit on the model. This is none too pleasing if it ruins many hours of careful work.

If you want specific decals for your model, it is unfortunate that we do not have as many specialist manufacturers as aircraft modellers do. There are really only two sets of decal sheets. Verlinden produce 1/35 rub-down or dry decals. More conventional water-slide decals are the original Almark series, now re-printed and available from E.D. Models in the UK. These are mainly for 1/76th but there were some 1/35th as well. One of your best bets is to keep all the spare decals from your kits. Most models these days provide a variety of finishes for you to choose from. Keep all the spares and you will find yourself with an excellent source to draw from. This applies equally to kits in both large and small scales, such as Fujimi, ESCI, Tamiya and Italeri.

8 REFERENCE AND RESEARCH

Any series modeller must undertake some sort of research. Many, including me, find it a problem choosing between buying books or new models. What I would like to do is to give you some idea of what is, and has been, available that you should find useful.

My own dream as a researcher would be to be able to travel to the various parts of the world to see and photograph the old battlefields, discover what wrecks are still there, either lost in a wood or rusting away on a Pacific Island. To be able to visit the various museums and collections around the world to see just what does still exist. I suppose in particular that I would most of all like to see the collection at the Aberdeen Proving Ground in the USA; then there is the pre-positioned weapons depots in Europe; the tank graveyards of the Middle East, or tank parks in the Soviet Union. Unfortunately, I am, like most people, with a wife and family and a mortgage that have to be maintained, so the money does not exist to ever meet these ambitions.

This means that we have to rely on a multitude of publications from a multitude of authors, all of whom have different ideas of what is most interesting. Then as the years go by, so more information is released, or new evidence is found, that can change what has gone before.

Books

For the modeller, reference books are essential, but they are not cheap. The question therefore is just what books to buy. I believe primarily that those containing a large number of photographs are the most useful for modellers. Equally, many of these concentrate on either a particular vehicle or on a particular theatre of war. The 'Tanks Illustrated' series from Arms & Armour Press is especially useful as well as being good value for money. Many of the titles explain their restricted subject matter well – *The Battle of the Bulge, D-Day Tank Battles, Allied Armour in Italy*, etc. Only slightly more expensive, and available in both soft and hard covers, are the books from Squadron-Signal in the USA. These are among the finest books of all for modellers, as they include full colour artwork which is superb and full of inspiration, based on fact. They also mix a super selection of black and white photographs with well-informed text. The ideal modellers reference. Titles produced, some also available through Arms & Armour Press, are: *Panzer Colours, 1, 2 and 3*; *Armour on the Eastern Front*; *British Tank Names and Markings: D-Day to Berlin*; *Armour in Vietnam*; *Armour in Korea*; *S.S. Armour and Blitzkreig*. Still with Arms & Armour Press, the German AFV enthusiast should have the *Encyclopedia of German Tanks*.

I always look for new and interesting photographs but do not ignore the text. The atmosphere of a model relates to the atmosphere of actually having been somewhere. Watch out for books whose written accounts give an insight into a particular scenario. For example, of huddling against the cold and mud of the Eastern Front; sheltering under apple trees in the Normandy countryside while morters burst around; or hiding among the close high hedges of the Bocage. It is important to keep some sort of balance.

Not too widely available now, Ian Allen produced a series of books with Armour "in Action" which are very good if you can get hold of them. Another small but excellent series are the *'War Albums'* produced by the German Magazine, 'Modell Fan'. These are collections of readers' photographs and they cover aviation, naval and armour subjects. There are some really useful and unusual shots which often provide great diorama ideas.

Patrick Stephens did produce a set of photograph books which included titles on *S.S. Armour*; *Armour on the Eastern Front*; *North Africa*; the *Balkans and North West Europe*. All these pictures were selected from the Bundesarchiv in West Germany. Fortunately for us, the Germans during WWII had photographs covering all their operations and a large proportion of them survived. Hence there are so many excellent pictures to be found in the Bundesarchiv.

For the modeller, Airfix Magazine once had a useful set of small guides, though many of them have since been left behind with newer information. One of the best ways to buy military books is still through the Military Book Society, run by W.H. Smith, with discount prices and a regular newsletter that keeps you up to date with what is available. Attractive introductory offers are often widely advertised.

There is an ever growing list of titles available today, but it is a pity that so many modellers have missed some of those early publications. An excellent series came from Almark publications. They had a wide variety of titles, many of which were useful to AFV modellers. There were items such as American Camouflage and Markings, British Vehicle Markings, Wehrmacht Divisional Signs, German Engineer Equipment, Waffen SS, German Camouflage & Marking, among others. Written by well known authors like Terry Wise, Chris Ellis and Terry Gander – packed full of useful bits and pieces. The problem today is obtaining them of course. Other than at local shows and model clubs, it is a good idea to keep an eye open for second hand bookshops. There are a number who specialise in military books and who regularly advertise in the modelling press. If you get the chance, visit one and have a good browse round. You can often find some useful bargains.

For the many modellers interested in the German equipment of WWII, then Ducimus books once produced the *Wehrmacht Wheeled Vehicles Directory.* Edited by Chris Ellis, this contained information from technical manuals that usually had one illustration of a type and then details that included height, width, length measurements among others, such as length of wheelbase.

From this you can work out your own scale measurements and make up your own conversions and scratch builds. It includes trucks and trailers for a variety of uses, such as telephone exchanges, command vehicles, fuel trucks, etc.

Finally, while you are unlikely to find the older books do not forget to try your local library. If you cannot afford to buy a book every time you need one, remember you can find them through the library and they will obtain one for you even if it is not normally held there.

Perhaps the moral is to always keep an open mind and look at any book you see, anywhere. Assess it for yourself as to whether it meets your needs and then decide whether or not to buy it, depending on its value. By doing so regularly, you will often find some unexpected bargains. For those of you interested in AFV crew uniforms, they appear in a variety of odd places, most particularly publications that have included some are *'Army Uniforms of WWII'* from Blandford Press and *'Tank 7 AFV*

Uniforms since *1916'* by Martin Windrow, published by P.S.L. Look out also for articles in the modelling press.

Scale Drawings

For the modeller, scale drawings are virtually essential, not only to enable you to make scratch builds and conversions, but also to check new models against. We are fortunate to have some excellent ones available. Some of the early drawings were faulty, and the product of some guess-work rather than the more concrete information which has become available since. If you can find them, there were an excellent set of booklets known as *'Bellona Military Vehicle Prints'*, which did much to pioneer the sort of material we have available today. Many of those early drawings, especially of soft-skins, were drawn by Mike Conniford among others.

There are also some excellent individual sets of drawings available. One of the largest list available is from Geoff Lacey, who covers WWI, WWII and modern vehicles, all to a constant 1/76th scale. Many of you may have seen his work in a number of publications and, indeed, I am grateful for his work in providing the Horsch featured earlier, the mobile church and Monty's caravan also featured here. Geoff is a marvellous example of our hobby, being someone who produces first-rate work even though it is not his full-time occupation. The drawings can be used for simple kit conversions or full scratchbuilds, and indeed some people collect them in their own right.

Another long standing producer of drawings is John Church, who has another large list covering allied vehicles. Each of these draughtsmen has their own recognisable style, and both are commonly used as reference by a number of the resin producers.

A third set is available from Model Transport, drawn by Trevor Claringbold. This is a relatively small list, but, as well as being of good quality, they are available in both 1/76th and 1/87th scales. So for those of you with interests in these scales, I have two more potential projects for you to try, with the 150mm SIG on PzII here, in 1/76th, and a Bedford QL in 1/87th. Again, my thanks to Trevor for providing the drawings that are included here.

MAFVA (Model Armoured Fighting Vehicles Association)

For any modeller interested in military vehicles, then MAFVA is for

A good 1/76 entry at a MAFVA competition in 1987. Many fine examples of the hobby can be seen at these meetings.

you. It has been established since the 1960's and it coincided with the popularity of 1/76th scale, so this is still the Association's most favoured scale. Nevertheless, whatever your favoured scale, this is the way to meet other people with the same interests and to exchange information and ideas. Membership is still very reasonable and it includes the bi-monthly publication 'Tankette'. This contains news, letters, reviews, scale drawings and vehicle features. It is organised into local branches, which hold regular meetings and competitions, leading to the annual National competitions. By attending this and local meetings, you can pick up lots of hints and ideas from having seen something and then being able to directly ask the modeller about it. The London Branch even produces its own magazine, 'Challenger'. It can only be good for the hobby that we should get together and encourage each other.

If you would like to join, and get further information on MAFVA, you will find the address at the end of this book.

The Modelling Press

The most readily available source of information is undoubtedly model magazines. Available from any local newsagent, here you will find all the up to date information on new products plus a great deal of original research material. The first real magazine for modellers was Airfix Magazine, and that in turn started on Military Vehicles in 1963. It was of course an aid for the Airfix Company in selling their products. Those early AFV conversions were where many of us began our interests, and where most pioneering work was done. I am sure I am not the only one who regularly read the articles from Chris Ellis and Gerald Scarborough, and was encouraged to have a go myself.

It was in January 1971 that 'Military Modelling' Magazine came along. Now it is among the world's leading hobby publications and has covered a huge variety of subjects over the years. For the vehicle enthusiast there have been features on unit histories, markings, AFVs and soft-skins, WWI to the present day, and conversions and scratch-builds in 1/35th and well as 1/76th scale.

On top of all that, the advertisements and reviews include details of the latest products, and most importantly, where to buy them. These products, be they vehicles, figures, scenery or books, come from all over the world and are normally not available in just a local model shop. Fortunately there are a number of specialist shops dealing with Mail Order, plus the ever growing number of small manufacturers who market their own products. In the UK we are very fortunate to have a number of shops who not only stock the usual kit ranges, but they have managed to obtain a number of the resin and metal products from some smaller producers. Mot notable in my opinion are the Harrow Model Shop, E.D. Models in Birmingham, and Wings & Wheels, Bath. These and others are listed in the Appendix. In other parts of the world Verlinden, Letterman & Stok in the USA and Yoshio Ohwada in Tokyo, Japan have also managed to stock some interesting selections.

Most modellers have some sort of limitation on their funds and I am no exception. So, with the continuous release of new products on the market with models, tools, books and scenery all competing for your money, the review columns serve an important purpose in providing some sort of judgement on these products to help you choose where to spend your money. But can I stress that you choose. Each one of us has our own views and that is the way it should be. Reviews should be seen as an informed guide but not necessarily the last word.

I value my magazine collection as a mine of information. If you ever have the opportunity to buy back-copies, then I urge you to do so, but do hunt around. They can often be found in local second-hand book shops at very reasonable prices. I have also heard of people who just cut out the features they are interested in and throw out the rest. I would never do that, because your interests may well widen as years go by, and you will long regret ever using those scissors.

I mentioned Almark publications earlier. Back in the early

Repainted in recent years, the Bovington King Tiger is one of the fifty built with the Porsche turret. Alongside are the other heavyweights, Panther and Tiger. (Photo: Courtesy of the Tank Museum).

A useful shot, taken some years ago, showing not only the size of the Jagdtiger at Bovington, but also the zimmeritt pattern, and clear areas for track guards and spare track shoes.

seventies, they produced a monthly magazine called 'Modelworld' (no relation to the recent one) which lasted for just two years. There was a lot of good information in it, and if you ever notice any, take a look.

It is strange how things turn full circle. It was Airfix who first released a real modellers' magazine, obviously to promote their own products. Now one of the most recent publications comes from Tamiya, though produced in the UK. Content for the Military Modeller is limited, however, as we share it with motorbikes, radio-control cars and aircraft. Nevertheless, it shows the revival in the modelling hobby and the support we are getting from one of the major manufacturers. There is one other hint I would pass on. Keep an eye open for publications from abroad. I particularly like to look at the ones from the USA. There is a lot going on and a number of alternative products available, which could well produce something of interest. I believe in examining as many alternatives as possible, then deciding which bits you want to make use of. 'Fine Scale Modeller' proves useful, but I can never get hold of the American Military Modeller magazine.

Museums

If you want information and details about a particular vehicle, then

Duxford's Jagdpanther, with three colour camouflage and the remains of a different pattern zimmeritt to that on Bovington's Jagdtiger.

A standard Beaverette in a good paint scheme at the Imperial War Museum collection at Duxford.

This American M7 is pictured at the Royal Artillery Museum, Rotunda, Woolwich.

A detail shot, showing the two-layer gun shield on a Pak 40 at the Royal Artillery Museum, Rotunda, Woolwich.

the best solution is to look at the real thing. There are a number of individuals and preservation societies who restore and maintain military vehicles. This is a subject all on its own, and too much to go into here. I would suggest you visit any rallies you can, equipped with a camera and plenty of film. But the most accessible source must be the museums that exist around the world.

In the UK, many museums have a few vehicles in their collections but the best two must be the Tank Museum at Bovington Camp in Dorset, and the Imperial War Museum Collection at Duxford in Cambridgeshire. I will come back in a moment to the large private collection belonging to A.F. Budge. The Tank Museum has around 140 vehicles exhibited, from WWI to the present day. It is useful to see them together, as you can get the correct impression of the relative sizes. From the small Panzers I and II up to the mighty King Tiger. Indeed, their King Tiger was a relative rarity, it is one of the few that mounted the Porsche turret.

The dirt and oil staining from the exhaust are clear on this well-used JSIII.

Morris Bofor's quad in a spotless condition at the Budge collection.

Both their Jagdtiger and a Stugg III also still have the remains of their Zimmeritt anti-mine coating. Interestingly they are also applied in different patterns. Other vehicles to remember are the Duplex-Drive Sherman, with the wading screen raised, and the prototye tank, Little Willie.

The Tank Museum also has other useful services. If you want photographs of any part of a vehicle in the collection, either inside or out, then for a reasonable fee they will do them for you. On top of that, they have a large photographic library covering the equipment of many nations other than Britain. Alongside, the document library is also available to the public, with many technical manuals, diagrams, stowage details and books. Copies of the photographs and photocopies of plans/diagrams are again available at very reasonable prices. Finally, we should be grateful for the work put into so many publications by the Curator, Lt. Col. George Forty and Chief Librarian, David Fletcher.

A Duxford, the Imperial War Museum has a fascinating collection that includes many military vehicles alongside their military and civil aircraft. Here there is the room to do things like have an erected VI missile launching ramp. Among a variety of interesting vehicles, you will find a Conqueror (a runner), a Dorchester ACV, and SU100 and a fine assortment of artillery and anti-tank guns. Of particular interest are Monty's three caravans which were moved up there from the Imperial War Museum, South Kennington site, and one single shell, a practice round from the Giant German Gustav 800mm railway gun.

A couple of other places here that are well worth a visit include the Royal Artillery Museum at the Rotunda in Woolwich. Here you will find a wide variety of artillery pieces, including an M7 Priest, an M12 155mm SP, an Honest John Transporter/launcher, German 75mm Pak 40 and Soviety 76mm gun, as well as a good

An interior shot of the Budge collection's JSU 152. Colours vary with white, grey, black, rust and basic dirt.

This M5 ½ track is seen on the 4th July display at the Patton Museum of Cavalry and Armour at Fort Knox. (Photo: Courtesy of the Patton Museum).

selection of British Army guns. Then the Museum of Army Transport at Beverley, North Humberside. Among interesting exhibits here you will find Monty's Rolls Wraith, which was landed over the beaches in Normandy for him, plus a Weasel, Buffalo and others.

Though not a museum, we have heard a lot about an ever growing private collection with A.F. Budge in Nottinghamshire. They do have one open weekend each year, but are otherwise not generally open to the public. They have gathered a very unique collection, which includes items obtained in the Middle East, and the first JSIII in the UK, a PT76, Israeli M48 and an unusual Egyptian conversion of the T34/85 to mount the Soviet 122mm D30 howitzer.

Moving to the USA most will know Fort Knox for the US Gold Reserve, but it is also the home for the Patton Museum. Here they have a large number of exhibits, some in the grounds and some in the museum buildings, plus a good number in storage. Here you will find Patton's Limousine, now fully restored after the crash which killed him, among other Patton memorabilia. Another unique item is a surviving Panther II.

A special point about the Patton Museum is that they try to keep the vehicles as runners, and have a popular display on the 4th July each year. They have around 300,000 visitors a year and the number is still climbing. Still in the USA there is the main collection at the Aberdeen Proving Ground in Maryland. Here there is a huge variety of equipment on display, both vehicles and artillery. One particular exhibit must be the 28cm 'Leopold' railway gun as modelled by Hasegawa. I must be honest and say this is the one place that heads my list of places to visit. Oh, to be let loose there with my camera and a good supply of film!

Prototype Bradley IFV now seen in the collection at Aberdeen Proving Ground, Maryland. (Photo: Courtesy of Miltra).

Useful modelling details can often be found in the photos of recovered wrecks. This Churchill AVRE was on the Warminster ranges, pictured here by 'After the Battle', and featured in 'Wheels and Tracks', No. 15. (Photo: Courtesy of 'After the Battle' publication).

Soviet T55s on the march. (Photo: Courtesy of Soviet Military Review).

Manufacturers' advertising often produces useful photo references for modellers. This is the LAV25TOW vehicle. (Photo: Courtesy of Emerson Electric).

Elsewhere there are good collections, at Saumur in France and the Australian War Memorial collection. Recently come to our attention has been a museum outside Moscow. It is not open to the public, but seen on a video and with a recent photograph release, a mystery has been answered. The world's largest ever tank, the German Maus, still lives in one piece. It was believed for

A useful detail shot of the Czech RM70. (Photo: Courtesy of the Soviet Embassy).

years that both completed prototypes were destroyed by the retreating Germans. It now seems that the one fully completed turret survived, as did the second hull. Captured by the Russians, they have put the two together, and the Super Tank lives on after all. The moral of this story is that examples of many vehicles, both common and rare, still survive. It is just that they are not all in the same place. Be prepared to hunt around.

An excellent source of information for modellers and historians alike appears in the magazine 'Wheels & Tracks', from 'After the Battle' publications. Published quarterly, it contains information from all round the world. It gives details and photographs from rallies, collections and museums. This is where David Fletcher released his new information on Maus in Russia. On top of this research information, it contains many photographs of old, unrestored, vehicles found in various places around the world and often the same thing in its restored state. There are lots of things for the modeller to pick up from these and I find it a valuable source for details.

General

In many countries you will find little museums, or the occasional vehicle mounted as a war memorial. Then there are the enthusiasts who restore and maintain old military vehicles. There are still a few places where vehicles can be found, which were left there some forty-odd years ago, although this category is now very small. From more up to date conflicts, the regular articles from

Vasko Barbic on the Middle East wars show how many wrecks still litter the deserts in that part of the world.

Add this to the number of private enthusiasts, who may be lurking anywhere, then it is worth carrying a camera with you either on holiday, or to local shows and rallies, or if you have a trip to an area you feel might be promising. I have done this a number of times and picked up some helpful shots. Examples such as a Chieftan on a transporter, stopped at a lay-by, enabled me to get some detailed shots. If I went over to France or Belgium, then my camera bag would definitely go with me.

There are news agencies and photograph museums that you can go to, but I treat them with care. They can be expensive, and unless you visit them yourself and pick the subjects you want, you may well be disappointed. The news agencies in particular tend to be very expensive in my experience, though some museums have a very reasonably priced photograph service. Choose carefully, especially if your funds are limited. Stick with the available books and magazines, or take original photographs yourself as and when the opportunities arise. You can try writing to various Embassies for information, but the reaction you get varies from very good (sometimes) to being totally ignored (often).

9   SUMMARY

So there you have it, a guide to the world of modelling military vehicles. I hope it has shown you just how huge a variety of models, information and accessories are lurking out there somewhere. There is plenty here to keep you going for a good many years. In writing my column in 'Military Modelling' magazine, I try to keep as up to date as possible, especially with new manufacturers. I try and contact those I hear of whenever I can, yet despite that there are still some who choose to ignore those enquiries. Frankly I do not understand why, as presumably they do want customers to buy their products. It does make me wonder therefore whether these people will treat their customers any better, and I will not pass on any unconfirmed information, unless I hear something definite from someone else.

We went through a period of decline in our hobby and that cannot be denied. Virtually all the major manufacturers have been bankrupt and have been bought out at one time or another. The backlash was the rise in smaller manufacturers, as modellers realised the only way to get a new model was to make it yourself. Thus the resin model grew in popularity. It was the use of polyurethene resin that revolutionised the whole scene. So much more detail and quality was suddenly possible and as it was so much easier to make-up, so a far wider group of people would buy them. It also saw the release of 1/35 conversion sets and, more recently, complete kits. Quality varies from poor to superb. The number of new producers is growing almost weekly and becoming ever more difficult to keep track of. Regrettably, some are bound to fall by the wayside, as you need to be a business as well. There have already been one or two, though their models live on as they have sold their moulds to others.

All in all, the fu`ure promise well for our hobby. What I have tried to do is give you an idea of just how much material is available to us.

If you like the SdKfz 251, here are just three variations on the early type chassis. There were many more variants on this same vehicle.

Experienced modellers may have found the existence of new items and ranges, have heard of things that were available before they started modelling, and finally I hope the beginner can find some ideas about how to find their way around this hobby.

I have tried hard not to tell you how to actually model. There are always alternatives, and I urge you to try them out and decide which you like most of all. The real secret to advancing your techniques is patience and experimentation. Never close your mind to anything, whether it is choice of scale, paint finish, or anything else. At the end of the day, it is a hobby, which is designed to give us some relaxation and enjoyment. It does not really matter how good or bad you are as a modeller, just that you enjoy it. There are a great number of excellent products for you to make use of and they are still growing. The results are showing as the major manufacturers are beginning to release not just new items, but limited editions of special interest to the enthusiast. Things look very bright for the future, and I urge you to widen your experiences and enjoy your modelling. This hobby has given me many hours of enjoyable relaxation. I hope it will provide as much for you. May I end by saying that while there are limitations to a book of this size, please feel free to ask questions. Personally, I will always be glad to try and help anyone. I cannot promise to have anything like all the anwers, but I will always be happy to try or simply to listen to other points of view.

APPENDICES

Modelling Organisations

IPMS/USA
P.O. Box 6369
Lincoln, N.E.
68506
USA

IPMS/UK
Membership Administrator,
Mr. J. Wright,
9 Pretoria Road,
Gillingham, Kent,
ME7 4ND

Gary Williams (President)
MAFVA,
15 Berwick Avenue,
Heaton Mersey,
Stockport, Cheshire,
SK4 3AA
England.

Publishers and Book Shops

After the Battle Publications
Church House,
Church Street,
London,
E15 3JA

Argus Specialist Publications/
Argus Books,
Wolsey House,
Wolsey Road,
Hemel Hempstead,
Herts.
HP2 4SS

P.S.L. Ltd.,
Denington Estate,
Wellingborough,
Northants,
NN8 2RQ

Arms & Armour Press Ltd.,
Link House,
West Street,
Poole, Dorset,
BH15 1LL

Squadron Signal Publications,
1115, Crowley Drive,
Carrollton,
Texas 75011–5010
USA

Osprey Books,
27a Floral Street,
London,
WC2E 9DP

Albion Scott Ltd.,
51 York Road,
Brentford
Middx. TW8 0QP

History Bookshop,
2 Broadway,
London,
N11 3DU

W.E. Hersant Ltd.,
228 Archway Road,
London,
N6 5AZ

Sky Book International,
48 East 50th Street,
New York,
N Y 10022,
USA

Model Stockists and Producers

Gramodels,
73 Castleton Avenue,
Wembley,
Middlesex,
England.
Also holds Akita etched brass vehicle accessories.

Pak 43 Models
Lynn Hayward,
445 Edgware Road,
London,
W2 1TH

Cromwell Models,
Regency House,
22 Hayburn Street,
Partick,
Glasgow, G11 6DG

Harrow Model Shop
190–194 Station Road,
Harrow,
Middlesex.
Holds Jacklex, GAS, Ahketon, Gramodels
and Minitanks plus all major manufacturers.

E.D. Models,
64 Stratford Road,
Shirley,
Solihull,
B90 3LP
Distributors of J.B. Models, K & K
Castings and stockists of Maquette D'Auzi,
Replica, AEF Designs, ADV, On The Mark
and Alby.

Ernest Berwick Limited,
Lancaster House,
55 Upper Benefield,
Peterborough,
PE8 5AL
Stockists of Tonda Vac Forms and Airmodel
Vac Forms and resin AFV kits.

Ostmodels,
8 Kingswood Crescent,
Berridale 7011,
Tasmania,
Australia.

Accurate Armour,
7 Main Street,
Killearn,
G63 9AB
Scotland.

Platoon 20,
Model Figures & Hobbies,
Lower Balloo Road,
Groomsport,
Co. Down, BT19 2LU
N. Ireland.

Model Transport,
18 Bevan Way,
Aylesham,
Nr. Canterbury,
Kent.

Miltra
357 Uxbridge Road,
Rickmansworth,
Herts.,
WD3 2DT

Airmodel,
Frank Modellbau,
Obere Vorstadt,
21 D-7470, Albstadt 1,
West Germany.

Scotia Micro Models,
32 West Hemming Street,
Letham,
Angus, DD8 2PU
Scotland.

Lead Sled Models,
42 Belgrave Road,
Newtake,
Newton Abbot, Devon,
TQ12 4JP
England.

Petner Panzers
P.O. Box 1221
Bensalem
PA 19020–0844

Armourtec Scale Models
P.O. Box 51550,
Pacific Grove,
CA 93950–1550

Alby,
21 Rue de Blois,
La Ferte-Villeneuil
28220 Cloyes sur le Loir
France

Des Resin
27 Rue des hauts de bonne eau,
94500 Champigny Sur Marne,
France.

MHW Models Limited
46 Haworth Road,
Crossroads,
Keighley,
West Yorkshire,
BD22 9 DL
Stocks KMR, Spojnia, Tauro and DES resin.

Skytrex
28 Brook Street,
Wymeswold,
Nr. Loughborough,
Leics. LE12 6TU
Stocks Firefight 20,
Hinchcliffe, Dauco 1/300
and Action 200

Red Star,
1 Grange Road,
Barcombe,
E. Sussex,
BN8 5AU

Quality Castings
P.O. Box 11714,
Alexandria,
Virginia 22312,
U.S.A.

A.D.V.
19 rue Bel Air,
Verdes,
41240 Ouzover le Marche,
France.

A.G.L. Modelcrafts,
38 Harrison Road,
Worthing,
West Sussex,
BN14 8LS.

Historex Agents,
3 Castle Street,
Dover,
Kent, England.
Stockist for Verlinden Products, Soveriegn, Barton Miniatures,
Belgo figures, Model Kasten tracks.

Ahketon,
12a, Olds Approach,
Byfleet Industrial Estate,
Tolpits Lane,
Watford. Herrs.
Produces Ahketon and Lyzards Grin.

S. & S. Models,
3 Dewar Close,
Burnham on Sea,
Somerset.

Fent-O-Res,
23 Avenue Parade,
Accrington,
Lancs.

Milicast Glasgow,
990 Pollokshaws Road,
Shawlands,
Glasgow,
G41 2HA

Sovereign/Miniature Military
Models,
J Tassel,
4 Hawkbeck Road,
Rainham,
Gillingham,
Kent.

Mercator,
David Vanner,
104 Stanwell Road,
Penarth,
CF6 2LP

Perry Vacu Models,
Ged. O. Gracht 112,
2011 GW Haarlem,
Holland.

Yoshio Ohwada 5–12-69–1017
Yashio,
Shinagawa-Ku,
Tokyo 140
Japan.
Distributor for Model Kasten,
Maxim, Sunny & Leo

Continental Model Supplies
36 Gray Gardens,
Rainham,
Essex. RM13 7NH
1/87 Specialist.
Roco Minitanks, Trident,
Roskopf, Model Transport
and C.M.S.C. figures.

Wings and Wheels (Tyresmoke Products),
30 Westgate Buildings,
Bath,
BA1 1EF. Avon, England.
Distributors of Top Brass,
Promods, P & P Aeroparts
Piper Model Castings and
Miniature Armour Conversions.

Scale Link,
42 Appleby Close,
Twickenham,
TW2 5NA

In-Country Hobbies,
1618, W. Auburn Street,
MESA,
AZ 85201
USA

Armor Research Co.,
P.O. Box 8583
Cedar Rapids,
1A 52408,
USA

Heroics & Roxs.
Unit 12, Semington Turnpike,
Semington,
Trowbridge, Wilts.
BA14 6LB.

M.B. Models,
4242 Big Ben Ct.,
Charleston,
S.C. 29418
USA

On the Mark Models,
P.O. Box 663
Louisville,
CO 80027,
USA

A.P.C. Hobbies
Box 122,
Earlysville,
VA 22936
USA
Stock Miley conversions,
Harper Conversions and
A.P.C. resins.

G.A.R.E. Model s.n.c.,
P.O. Box 4233,
00182 Roma
Italia.

MMS,
26 Crescent Rise,
Luton,
Beds. LU2 0AU

A.E.F. Designs,
14413 E. 47th Avenue,
Denver,
CO 80230, USA

The Arsenal
1506 Lorraine Avenue,
Bellvue,
NE 68005
USA
Stock Accurate Armour, Des, ADV, Alby, KMR, Replica,
Monarch, Schmitt-vac, Airmodel, K & K,
Sovereign, Gunze-Sanyo.

Verlinden, Letterman & Stok
25 Cross Keys Center,
Florissant,
MO 63033,
USA
Stock Miniature Armour Conversions,
Top Brass, Verlinden Products, Schmidt
vac-form, Fairy Models, Airmodel Resins,
MB models, PP Aeroparts.

H. & S. Models,
Donald L Squire,
9546 Metro Street,
Downey, California,
90240, USA

G.H.Q./Mini figs.,
1/5 Graham Road,
Southampton,
SO2 0AX

Other useful addresses

Alec Tiranti,
70 High Street,
Theale,
Reading, Berks.
RG7 5AR
Suppliers of polyester resins, RTV moulding rubber,
low melt metals and Centricast Casting machines.

Humbrol Ltd.,
Marfleet,
Hull, HU9 5NE

Plastruct Inc.,
1020 S. Wallace Place,
Industry
CA USA 91748

Carrs Modelling Products,
Unit 5, Centre 88 Elm Grove,
Wimbledon,
London SW19 4HE.

Scale Plans

Trevor Claringbold,
18 Bevan Way,
Aylesham,
Kent, CT3 3DN,
England.

G.W. Lacey,
315a South Lane,
New Malden,
Surrey, KT3 5RR
England

J.B. Church,
Honeywood,
Middle Road,
Tiptoe,
Nr. Lymington,
Hampshire.
SO4 0FX

Museums

The Tank Museum
Bovington Camp,
Wareham,
Dorset
BN20 6JG

Patton Museum of Cavalry
& Armour,
P.O. Box 208,
Ft. Knox,
KY 40121–0208
USA

Imperial War Museum,
Duxford Airfield,
Duxford,
Cambridgeshire.

Imperial War Museum,
Lambeth Road,
London, S.E. 1.

Museum of Army Transport
Flemingate,
Beverley,
North Humberside.

Restoration Groups

Military Vehicle Trust
P.O. Box 6,
Fleet,
Hants., GU13 9PE
England.

Military Vehicle Collectors Club,
Box 33697,
Thornton,
Colorado 80233
USA

SELECT BIBLIOGRAPHY

How to Build Dioramas	Shep Paine	Kalmach Books
Modelling Tanks & Military Vehicles	Shep Paine	Kalmach Books
The Verlinden Way, Vol. I–VI	Francois Verlinden	Verlinden Productions
Panzer Colours 1, 2 and 3	Bruce Culver	Squadron Signal
The Modelmakers Handbook	Jackson & Day	Pelhams Books
Guide to Military Modelling	Ken Jones	Argus Books
German Artillery of WWII	Ian Hogg	A & A Press
British & American Artillery of WWII	Ian Hogg	A & A Press
WWII Military Vehicle Markings	Terry Wise	P.S.L.
Soviet Tanks & Combat Vehicles of WWII	Steve Zaloga	A.A. Press
Soviet Tanks & Combat Vehicles 1946 to The Present	Steve Zaloga	A & A Press

INDEX

Accurate Armour 52
Adhesives 69
ADV 53
AEF 57
Aeromodel 62
Ahketon 37
Airfix 11, 61
Airmodel 43, 56
Alby 42, 54
Armourtec 25
Aurora 47

Bandai 46
Barton Miniatures 57
Books 114

Cesare Gambari 61
Cromwell Modells 29

Des Resin 54

ESCI 16, 50

Fairy Models 55
Fent O Res 34
Firefight 20 44
Fujimi 27

GAS 40
GHQ 64
Gramodels 31
Gunze Sanyo 61

Hasegawa 41
Heller 41, 50
Heroics & Ros 64
Hinchliffe 37, 61
Home moulding 74
H S Models 39

Italeri 49

Jacklex 34
JB Models 29

KK Castings 33, 59
KMR 62

Lead Sled 36
Leo 59
Lyzards Grin 37

MAFVA 117
Maquette D'Auzi 44
Matchbox 28
MB Models 55
Miley Conversions 59
Milicast-Glasgow 32
Miltra 22, 41, 55
Miniature Armour Conversions 58
Miniature Military Models 51
MMS 43
Model Kasten/Maxim 59
Modelling Press 118
Model Transport 25
Monogram 61
Museums 120

Nichimo 50
Nitto 27, 50

On the Mark 61
Ostmodels 38

Pak 43 35
Peddinghams 57
Perry Vac Form 59
Petner Panzers 24
Platoon 20 35
PP Aeroparts 41
Promods 46

Quality Castings 21

Red Star 30
Resins 87
Revell 48

Roco Minitanks 18
Roskopf 23

S & S Models 33
Scale drawings 117
Scale Link 35, 51
Scotia Micro Models 64
Scratchbuilding 91
Skywave 64
Sovereign 51
Spojnia 51
Sunny 38

Tamiya 47, 48
Tauro 51
Tonda 56
Tools 72
Top Brass 57
Trident 26, 65

Vac Forms 91
Verlinden Productions 43,
60